D0921013

Creating Digital Collections

CHANDOS
INFORMATION PROFESSIONAL SERIES

Series Editor: Ruth Rikowski
(email: Rikowskigr@aol.com)

Chandos' new series of books are aimed at the busy information professional. They have been specially commissioned to provide the reader with an authoritative view of current thinking. They are designed to provide easy-to-read and (most importantly) practical coverage of topics that are of interest to librarians and other information professionals. If you would like a full listing of current and forthcoming titles, please visit our web site **www.chandospublishing.com** or contact Hannah Grace-Williams on email info@chandospublishing.com or telephone number +44 (0) 1993 848726.

New authors: we are always pleased to receive ideas for new titles; if you would like to write a book for Chandos, please contact Dr Glyn Jones on email gjones@chandospublishing.com or telephone number +44 (0) 1993 848726.

Bulk orders: some organisations buy a number of copies of our books. If you are interested in doing this, we would be pleased to discuss a discount. Please contact Hannah Grace-Williams on email info@chandospublishing.com or telephone number +44 (0) 1993 848726.

Creating Digital Collections

A practical guide

ALLISON B. ZHANG AND DON GOURLEY

Chandos Publishing
Oxford · England

Chandos Publishing (Oxford) Limited
TBAC Business Centre
Avenue 4
Station Lane
Witney
Oxford OX28 4BN
UK
Tel: +44 (0) 1993 848726 Fax: +44 (0) 1865 884448
Email: info@chandospublishing.com
www.chandospublishing.com

First published in Great Britain in 2008

ISBN:
978 1 84334 396 7 (paperback)
978 1 84334 397 4 (hardback)
1 84334 396 7 (paperback)
1 84334 397 5 (hardback)

British Library Cataloguing-in-Publication Data.
A catalogue record for this book is available from the British Library.

Typeset by Domex e-Data Pvt.Ltd.
Printed in the UK and USA.

Contents

List of figures and tables

Figures

Tables

About the authors

Allison B. Zhang is the Manager of the Digital Collections Production Center of the Washington Research Library Consortium (WRLC) located in Maryland. Prior to WRLC, she was the Project Coordinator for Connecticut History Online, a collaborative digital library project in Connecticut. She also worked in the University of Rochester Libraries as Electronic Resource Librarian and Digital Project Specialist. Allison has been involved in the field of creating digital collections for over eight years. She has written articles and a book, and given presentations on a variety of topics including file formats on the internet, designing and creating websites, cataloguing internet resources, metadata strategies, creating digital collections, managing digitisation projects, digital libraries, and so on.

Don Gourley is the Information Technology Manager for the Digital Humanities Observatory, a project of the Royal Irish Academy in Dublin. Previously, Don was the Director of Information Technology for the Washington Research Library Consortium. In addition to managing IT services, he served as the lead architect for a number of library information systems, such as a personalised portal for library patrons, an intra-consortium borrowing and document delivery service, and a repository for managing and preserving digital collections. Prior to WRLC, Don managed software projects and IT services at the Smithsonian Institution and the University of Maryland, and before that worked as a software design engineer with Hewlett-Packard. Don has written articles on a variety of subjects including digital library services, systems administration and open source software. He also teaches college courses in computer science and project management.

The authors may be contacted at the following:

Allison Zhang
E-mail: *zhang@wrlc.org*

Don Gourley
E-mail: *donald.gourley@gmail.com*

Preface

The purpose of this book is to provide a practical guide to creating digital collections by sharing our experiences and practices in digitisation and digital collection management. Our goal is to help librarians and archivists in special collections and archives to understand the process of creating and maintaining digital collections. We hope managers of digital collections will find this book useful for learning skills to manage digitisation projects and providing digitisation services. Technologists will find this book helpful to raise their awareness of the issues involved in these processes and the potential solutions to resolve technical problems. The book will also be useful for graduate students in library and information science who are interested in digital libraries.

Throughout this book, we will discuss the issues and practices that occur during each stage of the creation and management of digital collections. We will provide real examples and useful tips. Our focus is on best practices and case studies rather than research and theory. We will mainly discuss digitisation of still images. Digitisation of audio and video are beyond the scope of this book, although once digitised such content is very similar to digital image objects and much of the information about planning, content models, metadata and management will apply equally to digital content in all formats.

We will also address digital preservation, but as a practical rather than theoretical topic. We view digital preservation as simply one more component of basic digital asset management, applying the philosophy that we can only prepare for the future we can reasonably predict and ensure that the digital objects are preserved in a reliable and accessible manner through each of the incremental stages of their existence.

This book will walk you through each stage of creating and managing digital collections. The processes include:

- planning digitisation projects;
- selecting material to digitise;
- designing metadata and content models;

- creating digital content files and metadata;
- designing the user access interface;
- selecting digital collections management software and scanning equipment;
- documenting projects and reporting access statistics;
- staffing and training digital collections management staff.

At the end of each chapter, we will present a case study that will continue throughout the book. This case study describes our experience with the Digital Collections Production Center at the Washington Research Library Consortium, a shared digitisation facility that provides digital conversion, information technology and project management services for consortium members.

Introduction

There is no denying that a digital revolution has occurred during the late twentieth and early twenty-first centuries. The proliferation of digital information resources has transformed virtually every business and endeavour. Most people today are quite comfortable working with digital content and expect that their information needs can be met online. Libraries, museums and other cultural institutions are responding to those expectations by supplementing or replacing their physical holdings with electronic resources. They also recognise the importance of digitising material to provide online access to their collections.

As libraries produce and license increasing amounts of digital content, they must address many challenges in the organisation and management of information. Some of the challenges can be met by the traditional practices of librarianship, such as selection, organisation and cataloguing. Other challenges, however, are unique to the digital world, including digitisation techniques, data structures, data backup and refreshing, data transfer and digital asset management. The processes to create and manage digital collections are a combination of what librarians have always done, with some new practices related to the unique aspects of the digital world.

What are digital collections?

A digital collection is simply a set of related items that are in electronic form. We call these electronic items *digital objects*. The NISO Framework Advisory Group states that a digital collection 'consists of digital objects that are selected and organized to facilitate their access and use' (NISO, 2004). Thus a digital collection is analogous to the traditional special collections of archival material that libraries manage.

A digital object may contain an image, representing a photograph, a drawing, a manuscript, a postcard, a newspaper clipping or other visualisation. It may include a sound recording, representing a piece of music, a speech, a story telling, a radio broadcast, and so on. A digital object may have moving picture content, such as a video or animation. Its content may be text-based, such as a Word document, a PDF document, a website, a collection finding aid, and so forth. Digital objects can be viewed or accessed through a computer, either from a storage medium like CD-ROM or DVD or from a website or other networked resource. Therefore digital objects are also referred to as 'machine-readable' objects.

The electronic content of a digital object is usually stored as computer system files, although it may also be stored as objects in a database. Content is sometimes referred to as 'data' or 'bitstreams', to reflect the fact that when transmitted between computer programs or across a network the information is simply streams of digital data with no real association with storage. We will, however, refer to a data component in a digital object as a *content file*, where a file is an ordered sequence of bits, whether the bits are on a storage device or a communications channel.

Besides the content files, digital objects include information about the data. This information is called *metadata*, that is, data describing other data. Metadata in a digital object may typically include title, creator or author and other descriptive data elements. In their early and influential digital library framework, Kahn and Wilensky (1995) formally define a digital object as 'an instance of an abstract data type that has two components, *data* and *key-metadata*. The key-metadata includes a *handle*, i.e. an identifier globally unique to the digital object.' Thus, in order for us to consider something as a digital object, it must include in its metadata, at a minimum, some kind of data element that uniquely identifies this object. The digital object identifier is used to access the object electronically, for example on the internet or from a DVD or a CD-ROM using a computer. The identifier must therefore be unique within that electronic medium.

Digital objects are created in two basic ways. One method is to create an electronic facsimile of an original physical or 'analogue' item. This process is called 'digitisation' and includes, for example, scanning a photograph to a digital image or transferring an analogue audio recording to electronic media. Another way of creating a digital object is with a digital creation facility, such as using a computer to produce an electronic document like a Word file, an HTML page or a PDF document, or using a digital camera to produce digital photographs or video. Digital objects produced by a digital facility originally are called 'born digital' objects.

In this book we are primarily concerned with collections of digitised material, especially digital surrogates of library special collections' physical material. The objects in these digital collections, like those in the original library special collections, must be selected and organised. A digital collection usually has a theme or a subject, which is determined by the people who create the collection or from the heritage of its original format. The digital objects may be selected from a single original collection and reflect its subject. For example, the American University History Photographs and Print Collection (*http://www.aladin. wrlc.org/dl/collection/hdr?auhist*) contains historical photographs selected by the librarians in the American University Library from their early history special collections materials. Another example is the *Treasure Chest of Fun and Fact* digital collection (*http://www. aladin.wrlc.org/dl/collection/hdr?treasure*), which contains digitised copies of issues of the Catholic comic book in The American Catholic History Research Center and University Archives' *Treasure Chest of Fun and Fact* Comic Book Collection (i.e. those published between 1946 and 1972). A digital collection can also be selected from multiple physical collections and even include material from more than one institution.

An online set of one or more related digital collections is often known as a digital library. A digital collection, then, can be considered a digital library, although that term is usually reserved for larger sets of collections. Digital libraries are usually organised by collections, and the collections are related in that they are targeted towards a defined community or set of communities. Examples of digital libraries include American Memory (*http://memory.loc.gov/ammem/index.html*) created by the Library of Congress, the Colorado Digitization Project (*http://www.cdpheritage.org*) and the California Digital Library (*http://www.cdlib.org*).

Why create digital collections?

In her well-known report 'Strategies for Building Digitized Collections' Abby Smith (2001) points out that 'libraries usually identify two reasons for digitization: to preserve analog collections and to extend the reach of those collections'. These two motivations are often referred to as preservation and access.

Digitisation as a means of preserving the original is an expensive and ultimately futile proposition. In order to eliminate the need to view and handle the original, the digital facsimile must be of extremely high quality, requiring very expensive equipment, operator time and skills. Documents with difficult-to-read text will require manual transcription and markup, at additional cost. Three-dimensional objects require even more expensive equipment and multiple image views. Even then:

> digital surrogates can almost never be considered replacements for analog originals, which have intrinsic value and compared with which even the best-quality digital image represents a loss of information – inevitably failing to convey the unique feel, scent, weight, dimension and patina of a physical object. (Besser, 2003)

However, digitisation may diminish the actual handling of originals, which is an 'indirect preservation effect' (Hughes, 2004):

> The use of scans made of rare, fragile and unique materials – from prints and photographs to recorded sound and moving image – is universally acclaimed as an effective tool of preventive preservation. For materials that cannot withstand frequent handling or, because of their value or content, pose security risks, digitisation has proved to be a boon. (Smith, 2001)

On the other hand, digital collections can increase awareness of the physical collections, resulting in greater demand for the originals. Librarians must continue to apply traditional processes to preserve the originals as best they can, rather than rely on digitisation to reduce that obligation.

We believe extending and improving access to special collections material is the primary reason to embark on digitisation projects. Libraries host many unique materials in the form of special collections. These collections may be in a certain form, on a certain subject, in a certain time period or geographic area, in fragile or poor condition, or especially valuable. Such materials are not allowed to circulate, and access to them may be restricted because of their condition. As digital technologies develop, the growing and persistent demand for more and more digital content arises (Lynch, 2002). Digitising these precious primary materials has become a strategic goal of many libraries, and those that recognise this objective are starting to move beyond specific digitisation projects to build an infrastructure for making digitisation an intrinsic part of their special collections and archival processes.

Even if digital surrogates can never completely replace originals, the digital format still has many benefits over the original physical form. Digital collections can be viewed from all over the world wherever internet access is available. Access can be provided at any time, rather than being limited to the specific operating hours of the library department. Researchers and students do not need to travel to various repositories to find the information. They can sit in their office or home using fingers to travel in the sea of information and to find valuable resources for their research. The digital objects can be downloaded, manipulated and studied. Many people can access the digital collections simultaneously so they do not need to wait for a loaned-out item to be returned. High-quality or specialised imaging can reveal previously indiscernible details that might be useful in the conservation and/or analysis of original artefacts. (National Library of Australia, year unknown). In summary, digital collections provide enhanced functionality, convenience, and aggregation of collections that are physically dispersed, as well as greatly expanded reach (Smith, 2001).

The benefits of providing electronic access to digital collections, particularly on the internet, have prompted many libraries, museums and cultural institutions to assign dedicated staff or entire departments to digitisation work. Digitisation presents many challenges regarding staff, skills, technology, standards, and so on, but perhaps the greatest challenge is funding. To address these challenges, some institutions are starting to collaborate with other institutions and to create an organisational structure and technical infrastructure to make digitisation a core part of the institutional mission. The Digital Collections Production Center described in the case study throughout this book is an example of a collaborative effort to provide affordable and reliable digitisation and digital collection management services to support that mission.

Case study: the Digital Collections Production Center

The Digital Collections Production Center (DCPC) at the Washington Research Library Consortium (WRLC) is one of the many digitisation facilities at research and higher education institutions around the world. The WRLC is a library consortium serving eight academic institutions in the Washington, DC metropolitan area. In 2001, the WRLC received a National Leadership Grant from the federal Institute of Museum and Library Services (IMLS) for a two-year project to build the DCPC and provide digital conversion services for the WRLC member libraries.

The goal of this project was to create a shared facility to consolidate project management, information technology and digital conversion experience in a production environment (Payne, 2001). Major tasks of the project included hiring staff, selecting and purchasing equipment and software for digital conversions, selecting systems to manage and deliver digital objects, scanning materials selected from four testing collections, designing and creating Dublin Core metadata to describe digital objects and encoding finding aids in Encoded Archival Description (EAD) format. The outcome of the grant-funded project was a collaborative technical and organisational digital collections infrastructure, including a set of tools to facilitate the creation of digital collections, documentation describing the process and procedures, guidelines providing instructions and guidance for the member libraries to develop their digital collections, several experimental digital collections, and a finding aids database (Zhang and Gourley, 2003).

Payne, the Executive Director of WRLC, pointed out in the grant proposal that the organisational structure, procedures, technical and workflow guidelines and partner relationships which WRLC seeks to define through this project should serve for other library consortia or distributed library systems which seek to collaborate on digitising projects (Payne, 2001). Through several years of operation, the DCPC has developed a stable production-level organisational structure for building and sharing digital collections. A great number of digital resources representing the unique collections from the WRLC member libraries have been made available to students, researchers and the general public. The procedures, workflow guidelines and technical infrastructure developed by the DCPC have proven to be effective and flexible. The services provided by the DCPC have proven to be valuable to the member libraries, and in late 2003 at the end of the IMLS-funded project, the libraries agreed to incorporate the DCPC into the consortium's core services and operating budget.

Throughout the book we will relate the chapter topics to the DCPC, including how the DCPC addressed the requirements and issues that arose, the mistakes that were made and how they were corrected, and the practices and processes that were developed and have proven useful for future projects.

2

Planning and managing digitisation projects

Successful digitisation projects are the products of successful planning. Planning digitisation projects strategically will improve the quality of the project, assure a smooth and efficient workflow, and also reduce the overall cost of the project. A methodical approach will save time, effort and resources in the long run. Therefore, an 'investment in this kind of planning will be amply repaid over the life of the project' (NINCH, 2002).

According to Tanner (2001), at least one-third of technology-based projects that fail do so because of inadequate project management and control. Another third fail because objectives are not defined or the people involved in the project are not familiar with the project's scope and complexity. Most of the rest fail because of problems with communications. Only a small percentage of failed technology projects do so as a result of problems with the technology itself. Tanner concludes, 'an essential element to project planning is to ensure that the purpose of the project (or vision) is clear and is communicated to all involved'.

Knowing the purpose of the project and specifying clear goals is essential to success. Taking time to talk about issues and outcomes with people involved in the project will help clarify the project goals. Questions to ask and discuss include: What are the potential outcomes of the project? Does this digitisation project help the institution achieve its goals and missions? What are the target audiences? What should the final product look like? What are reasonable expenses for this project? What resources are available in-house? What kinds of funding are available?

Key components of a digitisation cycle

All digitisation projects follow a similar lifecycle through development and delivery. Understanding the steps involved in a digitisation project lifecycle will help in producing a realistic project plan. The key components of a digital imaging production cycle involve:

- selecting material;
- designing metadata;
- digitising material;
- creating metadata;
- designing presentation;
- delivering and disseminating the digital content;
- maintaining the collection.

For each stage, the planning process needs to identify:

- what work needs to be done;
- how the work will be done;
- who will do the work;
- how long it will take to do the work;
- how much it will cost (including equipment and staff time) to finish the work.

We will discuss the details of each of the lifecycle stages in the following chapters. Table 2.1 presents a brief list of what might be involved in each stage.

Project management

The best practices for managing a digitisation project depend on the scale, various stakeholders, available resources and other factors that vary from project to project. However, several basic project management practices are critical to the success of all digitisation projects, including leadership, communication, documentation, workflow planning and prototyping.

Table 2.1 Brief list of tasks involved in each stage of the digital image production cycle

Stage	Tasks involved	Tools and techniques	Staff involved
Select material	Develop criteria Select materials Prepare materials	Local selection criteria Best practices Guidelines	Special collection Archives Subject librarians
Design metadata	Analyse material Outline display features Determine relations between items Design file naming convention Design structural metadata	Best practices Metadata standards Project requirements	Metadata specialist Programmer Presentation designer
Digitise material	Assign correct filenames Image quality control Image processing	Best practices Guidelines	Scanning technician
Create metadata	Create template Create records Assign subject headings	DCMS Metadata schemas Controlled vocabulary	Cataloguer or metadata specialist Subject specialist Special collection and archives
Design presentation	Design navigation Configure the presentation system Design graphics Design homepage	DCMS Markup languages Accessibility standards	Graphic designer Web designer Metadata specialist Programmer
Deliver and disseminate staff content	Publicise the collection Notify potential users	Search engines Library catalogues Websites	Project manager Special collections and archives Public services librarian Webmaster
Maintain the collection	Monitor software and hardware Backup data Migrate data and systems	DCMS	Project manager Systems administrator Programmer Webmaster

Leadership

Leadership is a critical element for completing a digitisation project successfully. Each digitisation project must have a manager or a management team who takes responsibility for all aspects of the project. The manager must be knowledgeable about all components and stages of digitisation, standards and best practices, and issues and potential problems related to digitisation. But in order to be a good leader, the manager must also be able to inspire, motivate and influence the people involved in the project. It is often said, 'you lead people and manage things'. A good project manager must, of course, do both.

One of the most effective ways to lead is by example. Setting goals, establishing a project plan with milestones, developing procedures, guidelines and workflow, creating and ensuring communication channels, reviewing progress, controlling quality, involving all stakeholders at the right time and place during the project, directing project implementation, and so forth, are responsibilities of project management that should set the tone for how a project will be implemented.

Leadership also involves being able to anticipate and plan for issues that may arise during the project. Project management should identify the risks and uncertainties that might affect the project and develop contingency plans for dealing with them. In addition, good project managers must be aware of the larger needs of their organisation and stakeholders so they can lead their projects towards those goals and suggest future projects that are strategically important.

Communication

Good communication is also key for successful project management. As Chapman points out:

> Good management is largely an act of communication. If the people who work on the project understand the desired outcomes, they will provide better services; they will be aware of their individual contribution and how it relates to what others are doing; they will know why they are digitizing collections (the vision thing); and, perhaps most importantly, they will be better at recognizing when things go wrong. (Chapman, 2000)

Communication may take many forms and utilise different media and channels. Good communication is a prerequisite to many other project management practices such as leadership and documentation. Communication must be managed to ensure that necessary information is gathered and disseminated appropriately.

Any digitisation project, whether small or large, collaborative or institutional, will involve a group of people with different responsibilities. For example, an archivist or special collections librarian will need to select materials; a technician or student worker will scan the materials; a metadata specialist or a cataloguer will create the metadata, and a webmaster will design the presentation. The information technology (IT) staff will need to provide server, storage and other infrastructure. Although in small institutions, one person may carry multiple duties, it is rare that one person has all the skills needed for a digitisation project. If a project involves more than one person, there must be good communication to let people involved know their duties and desired outcomes, when they should accomplish their task, how their work relates to other people's work, and who to contact if they have any questions or problems related to the project.

Large collaborative projects often form several committees to take responsibility for different aspects of the project. For example, a management committee is responsible for managing the project, obtaining funding, hiring or assigning staff, and making decisions on major issues of the project. A selection committee is responsible for developing selection criteria and selecting material for digitisation. A technical committee is responsible for selecting software and hardware, designing the system architecture, establishing technical specifications, resolving technical problems and issues, and so on. A metadata committee is responsible for assuring the project follows relevant metadata standards and best practices, developing guidelines for creating metadata records, etc. A web design committee may be responsible for designing web presentations for the project, specifying accessibility requirements, and ensuring compatibility with site standards.

Communication between technical and non-technical staff supporting a digitisation project requires special attention because they often come at digitisation projects with different perspectives, training and ways of expressing themselves. As Umbach (2001) notes, 'talking to technical staff is an art in itself'. An article by Rossmann and Rossmann explains:

> much like any successful relationship, when technology staff and library staff take the time to understand how the other person views the world and keep open, clear channels of communication they can create a much more harmonious relationship than one where one's own needs always take priority. (Rossmann and Rossmann, 2005)

Digitisation projects are technology-based projects and without contributions from IT staff, either in-house or outsourced, it is impossible to succeed. The most important factors in communicating with IT staff are to articulate desired results as clearly and specifically as possible, and to collect and document information that IT staff need to understand those requirements. IT staff need to be aware that non-technical staff often have trouble visualising how an application will function. Whenever possible they should provide pictures, screen or webpage mock-ups and system prototypes to help non-technical staff evaluate whether IT solutions will be effective in a digitisation project.

Documentation

Good project management includes documenting detailed information about the project, as:

> documentation of the choices your project has made can be a key factor in the long-term success of digitization efforts. Good documentation can offset the impact of staff turnover and allow future staff an ability to deal with digital collections created by their predecessors. (Western States Digital Standards Group, 2003)

Chapman discusses the importance of documentation:

> the project manager has done his or her job well if the people who worked on it had a satisfying experience and if the future manager(s) of the digital collection can easily interpret why things were created in a particular way and what needs to be done to maintain, or even to improve, these first-generation digital objects. (Chapman, 2000)

This documentation includes project plans, metadata guides, workflow and other process descriptions, system user guides, and data flow diagrams. Creating and maintaining documentation takes significant effort and time; sometimes it is more difficult to document a process or a task than to carry it out. However, spending time on documentation will provide benefits in the long run as digital collections are maintained and enhanced. In addition, if systems and processes are standardised across digitisation projects, less unique documentation will be required for each new project. We will discuss more details about how to document digitisation projects in Chapter 11.

Workflow planning

Digital object creation can be a complex and time-consuming task. Digital files need to be generated from the source material and possibly manipulated and processed. Descriptive, administrative and structural metadata must be created and somehow attached to the digital content to which it refers. And all of these tasks must be done in a consistent manner to ensure that all digital objects are of good quality and usability. It is project management's responsibility to plan the workflow of these tasks into the most efficient steps to guarantee the consistency and quality of the digital objects. This means knowing what to do in what order and making sure that the inputs for each step are available when that step is performed. Failure to plan the workflow steps properly will likely result in poor workflow, inconsistent results and time delays.

Good workflow planning also requires understanding the requirements and dependencies between different steps in the creation of a digital collection. For example, while it is obvious that metadata design should precede metadata entry, if a file naming convention is going to be used to identify relationships between digital objects, then structural metadata design may need to be done before scanning begins.

Prototyping

Prototyping is the process of creating a small-scale, incomplete model of the planned digital collection product. Prototyping with a pilot project allows you to go through the full lifecycle of the digitisation project to help design and plan the full-scale project. If possible, the pilot project should select a small amount of representative material and go through a full cycle of digitisation, that is, scanning, creating metadata, and making the content accessible on a test site. The prototyping process will help confirm the correct workflow, ensure image quality, improve metadata creation, identify potential problems or issues, and provide example digital products for review. The pilot collection may be discarded before building the full-scale digital collection, it may be a small useful collection on its own and published as such, or it may be the beginning of a production digital collection, which can be expanded incrementally after the prototype is evaluated.

Developing a project plan

No project should be undertaken without a solid, documented project plan. The project plan describes the intended result of the project, how and when it will be implemented, and what resources are needed to complete it. It is a tool for communicating the details of the project to all stakeholders and for periodically reviewing the actual project progress compared with the planned progress. The project plan is also useful during the ongoing management and maintenance of a digital collection, and for planning future projects.

A good project plan includes many components that answer the following questions:

- Project summary
  - What is the intended result of the project?
  - What is the scope of the project (including what is out of scope)
  - What is the strategic significance of the project?
  - Who are the stakeholders (including collaborators)?
  - What are the target audiences for using the digital collection?
- Resource requirements
  - Who will be working on the project (including how much of their time will be devoted)?
  - What equipment and software systems will be used?
  - What other IT infrastructure is the project dependent on?
- Timeline
  - When will specific activities commence and conclude?
  - When will major milestones occur?
  - What are the deliverables expected for each milestone?
- Workflow plan
  - What steps are involved in the creation of digital objects?
  - What order do the steps occur?
  - What are the dependencies between steps?
  - How will the data flow through the various steps?
- Communication plan
  - What information needs to be distributed?

- What methods and technologies will be used to convey information?
- What specific documents will be produced?
- What is the frequency of communication (including documents, meetings, etc.)?

■ Test plan
- How will the project results (i.e. digital collections) be tested?
- When will testing occur?
- How will image and metadata quality be evaluated?
- What tools will be used to assist in testing?

■ Risk factors
- What risks are likely to affect the project?
- What are the relative likelihoods of different risks occurring?
- What impact could each risk have on the project?
- What responses are planned should the highest likelihood or potential impact risks occur?

For large projects that involve many people and tasks, it may be useful to use project management software to develop the project plan and track project status during the project. These tools are especially useful for developing the timeline in a hierarchical breakdown structure of tasks, describing dependencies between tasks, assigning resources to each task, and monitoring the progress and schedule of the tasks and milestones. The timeline can be displayed or printed in various formats, such as nested lists, dependency charts and network diagrams. Microsoft Project is a widely used project management program that includes all these features. For many projects, with more limited scope and resources, ordinary office productivity software, such as word processing, spreadsheet and drawing programs are sufficient for producing the project plan and other documentation required during the project.

Case study: DCPC's planning and management

Although the DCPC is a centralised facility for digital conversion and routinely implements digitisation projects, planning still plays a very important role in its operation.

The DCPC's planning process begins when a library has selected a collection for digitisation. During planning, the DCPC staff review materials and available information about the collection, define requirements for indexing, display and navigation, and design metadata based on the characteristics of the materials and structures of the collection. A number of planning documents are developed, including project agreement, rights and permission statements, material characteristics and scanning specifications, metadata schema, metadata templates and sample metadata records.

In addition, the planning process involves scheduling time and staff for the project (sometimes in conjunction with other projects to improve efficiency), communicating with staff in the WRLC IT department to discuss the support required for setting up systems, storage, and custom programming if needed.

The DCPC also works with libraries on projects where it may be more suitable to outsource the digital conversion to a service bureau, either because the materials are well-suited to batch processing or because they require specialised equipment (materials such as microforms, audio or video, or very large quantities of printed matter). In such cases, the DCPC provides the project management, design and descriptive metadata services, and can load the resulting digital objects into the ALADIN digital library (Payne, 2004).

In order to manage digitisation projects efficiently and properly, the DCPC has developed a number of procedures, including guidelines for handling and storing original materials and a procedure for receiving and safely returning the original materials. Workflows for each step of the digitisation and metadata creation process are documented in detail and checked regularly to ensure efficiency and quality. In the case when the owning library has funding or staff time available for metadata creation, the DCPC provides tools and instructions for the library staff to use. During each digitisation project, once a small number of items are digitised and related metadata made available, the DCPC designs and creates a prototype website for the owning library staff to review and provide feedback. This helps us to adjust techniques in scanning and image conversion and improve the quality of the metadata, if necessary. This also avoids making more mistakes in the later stage of the project when it is much more expensive to correct them. When a project is completed, the DCPC sends a summary of the project to the owning library, including statistics of scanned images and metadata records, starting and completion dates for each phase of the project, and special notes. This summary helps the library determine strategies and develop more efficient plans for future digitisation projects.

The computing support infrastructure at the WRLC is centralised. Responsibility for computer systems, disk and tape-storage units, programming, and all aspects of server operations lies with the IT department. The support of that department is essential to DCPC operations. IT staff provide expertise in software/server testing, installation and maintenance, custom programming, developing new tools and improving existing tools for creating and managing digital collections.

Communication with IT staff is an important aspect of DCPC management. Effective communications between the DCPC and the IT group are based on mutual understanding and trust. To help the IT group understand what is requested from the point of view of librarians or users, the DCPC staff always try to articulate their needs clearly and to find as much information as possible for the tasks they want to implement. Then they let them do their job. This partnership has resulted in the reliable delivery of quality services by both departments.

3

Selecting material for digitisation

Selecting material for digitisation is a complicated process that must balance several competing factors. As Vogt-O'Connor notes:

> selection involves choosing among a number of options using informed judgment and selection criteria. Good selection techniques ensure that resources are invested wisely in digitizing the most significant and useful collections at the lowest possible cost without placing the institution at legal or social risk. (Vogt-O'Connor, 2005)

Vogt-O'Connor also provides a very useful checklist for selection and evaluation of materials for digitisation.

Differences between selecting traditional material and selecting for digitisation

There is a wealth of literature on the subject of developing selection criteria for digitisation. Many institutions that have been engaged in digital library work for some time have developed selection criteria for their digitisation projects, usually in the form of written guidelines. Many of these selection guidelines have been published on the web, and indicate best practices for libraries that are just starting digitisation projects. Most guidelines list major factors such as research value, added value, legal restrictions, and technical feasibility as the primary considerations of selection criteria for digitisation.

In 2001, Abby Smith surveyed a subset of 'first-generation' digital libraries, that is, those that have been engaged in significant projects for a while and a few libraries that are just beginning to develop digitisation programmes. After reviewing selection criteria from major projects, she points out:

> the primary nontechnical criterion – research value – is a subjective one and relies on many contingencies for interpretation. What does it mean to say that something has intrinsic research value? Do research libraries collect any items that do not have such value? Should we give priority to items that have research value today or to those that may have it tomorrow? What relationship does current demand have to intrinsic value? Because the answers to these questions are subjective, the only things excluded under these selection criteria are items that are difficult to scan (for example, oversized maps) or things that are very boring or out of intellectual fashion. (Smith, 2001)

She concludes:

> While guidelines for technical matters such as image capture and legal rights management are extremely useful and should be codified, formal collection-development policies are still a long way off. (Smith, 2001)

Several years have passed since Smith's conclusion; the development of formal collection-development policies for digitisation is still underway. The questions she raises regarding the 'research value' as the primary nontechnical criterion may motivate librarians to think more carefully when developing a selection policy for digitisation.

One of the major issues that has not been discussed in depth is whether the selection criteria for digitisation and for traditional library materials should be the same. Some believe that selection for digitisation and selection of published materials is similar in some aspects and 'these same criteria should drive selection of traditional materials for digitization' (Cornell University Library, 2005). Others believe that:

> selecting materials for a digital project entails different factors than selecting print materials, such as legal issues and the high costs of digitization projects. In addition, the project team needs to determine if the materials to be digitised warrant the time and expense of transferring the digital files to new formats every few years as technologies change. (Lopatin, 2006)

Drawing from our experience, we have found that there are many differences between selecting traditional material and selecting material for digitisation. The major difference is that selecting material for digitisation is usually based on the collections and items the library already has. The library is re-selecting or repurposing the material rather than selecting new resources. This makes the selection process one of the most difficult tasks in the digital resources management lifecycle. (Hartman et al., 2005). Further differences are given below.

First, the meaning of research value for selecting traditional material versus material for digitisation may be different:

> because the methods of research used for digital materials differ from those used for analog, and the types of materials that are mined – and how – are also fundamentally different. Several large digitisation programs today are grounded in the belief that it is the nature of research itself that is 'repurposed' by this technology, and it is often surprising to see which source material yields the greatest return when digitzed. (Smith, 2001)

Second, the targeted audiences for a library's traditional collections are often different from those for digital collections. The collection development policy in academic libraries supports the local needs of the students, professors and researchers of the institution. In contrast, many large collaborative digitisation projects, especially federal government funded digitisation projects, require that the projects have national impact and that the content has broader research value. For example, the Connecticut History Online (CHO) project (*http://www.cthistoryonline.org/cdm-cho/index.html*) was a collaborative endeavour originally between three institutions in Connecticut funded by The Institute of Museum and Library Services. It was 'designed to help students in grades 7–12 build observation, analysis, and critical thinking skills by bringing primary resources into the classroom' (CHO, 2000); at the same time, one of its initial partners was the Thomas J. Dodd Research Center at the University of Connecticut, an institute that primarily serves scholars, researchers and students in higher education. Another example is the SMETE Digital Library, which aims to be 'the premier digital collection of resources and services for the nation and the world in SME&T [science, mathematics, engineering, and technology] e-learning' (SMETE Digital Library, 1999). Many of the SMETE Digital Library's participants are academic libraries who selected their materials for serving K-12 education.

Third, digitisation can be driven by demand for the resources, and in many digitisation projects, requested or anticipated use is a primary selection criterion for materials. For example, because of the large number of university schools and departments that could make use of the digitised posters, Temple University selected their First and Second World War poster collection as one of their pilot digitisation projects (Jerrido et al., 2001). The staff in special collections and archives departments know what materials and which collections generate the greatest user interest, and often propose digitising these collections first. Digitisation of such materials and collections not only provides simultaneous access for many users but also reduces the time and work that librarians need to do in handling requests, scheduling visit time, reproducing the originals, and otherwise satisfying the demands on the physical material.

Fourth, many digital collections are subject-oriented, where the selection is focused on the required subjects, sometimes in a specified time period. This is especially common in collaborative digitisation projects, which require selecting materials from separate physical collections to form a new subject-oriented digital collection. For example, the CHO project mentioned earlier in this chapter selected materials and collections from five participating institutions representing libraries, museums and historical societies. The CHO provides a comprehensive chronicle of events, people and places documenting social, business, political, educational, cultural and civic life in Connecticut and America. The materials selected cover the period 1760 to 2000 and come from five thematic categories: diversity, livelihoods, lifestyles, environment and infrastructure (CHO, 2001).

Fifth, selection of material for digitisation must consider the question of copyright and other legal and ethical restrictions that govern access to collections. In addition to copyright, restrictions may be required because of privacy, content or donor concerns. The rights and obligations of the library change significantly when material is reformatted or repurposed through digitisation and distributed over the internet. Whether or not the library has the right to reformat items and distribute them in limited or unlimited forms is a major consideration that is often hard to determine. Copyright ownership can be particularly difficult to identify. Meanwhile, many countries have extended the length of their copyright terms. Removing from consideration materials that are or might be under copyright is sometimes the only way to eliminate the risk of copyright infringement (Smith, 2001).

Sixth, technical feasibility is a unique and major issue when selecting for digitisation. Whether the existing technology and the in-house equipment can produce the desired results is one of the most important factors to be considered when selecting material for digitisation. For example, converting large maps to digital format requires a large-format scanner or a high-quality digital camera. It also requires zooming, panning and other functionality from the display software in order to make effective use of the digital images. This can be very expensive and very difficult for those institutions that do not have a large funding source, although the costs for supporting hardware and software are coming down. Still, in many cases, existing technology cannot produce the quality and results required for certain types of material, so those types of material must be excluded from consideration. It is important to remember that technical feasibility changes as digital technology is developed and becomes mainstream, so selection criteria must be periodically revisited.

Major considerations in developing selection criteria

There are no absolute rules to follow when developing selection criteria for digitisation. Each digitisation project is unique, has its own goals and purpose, and must satisfy specific organisational needs. Recognising how the selection criteria for digitisation projects differ from the selection criteria for traditional library collections helps identify the major issues that need to be addressed when selecting material for digitisation. These considerations include legal restrictions, value added by digitisation, target audiences and technical feasibility.

Legal restrictions

Legal restrictions and copyright assessments play a defining role in digitisation projects and must be addressed early in the selection process. If a proposed digitisation project involves materials that are not in the public domain and the library does not control the rights, permissions must be secured and appropriate fees paid. If permissions are not forthcoming, the materials cannot be reproduced and the focus of the project must change (Hazen et al., 1998).

Many experts suggest beginning the selection process by considering legal restrictions. Copyright and other legal restrictions are very complex, with many national variations, and will not be explored here in detail. Kenney et al. (2002) recommend two good resources to consult for copyright issues in the USA:

- 'When US works pass into the public domain' by the Professor of Law and Director of the Law Library at University of North Carolina at Chapel Hill (see *http://www.unc.edu/%7Eunclng/public-d.htm*).

- 'Copyright term and the public domain in the United States' by Peter Hirtle of the Cornell Institute for Digital Collections, which is specifically geared to archival and manuscript curators (see *http://www.copyright.cornell.edu/training/Hirtle_Public_Domain.htm*).

Value added by digitisation

According to Smith, 'in theory, a library would choose to digitize existing collection items only if it could identify the value that is added by digitization and determine that the benefits outweigh the costs' (Smith, 2001). In practice it is easy to identify value added by digitisation, but assigning a value that can be compared with the costs is much more difficult and sometimes impossible. As a selection criterion it is important to compare the relative added value for each candidate digitisation project. Examples of added value include:

- *Providing unrestricted and remote access to archival or special collections.* Many libraries host a large amount of historical materials in their archives and special collections. These are primary resources for researchers to study history and other subjects. The materials are often not made available to most library users because everyday use will damage fragile and deteriorating items. Converting them to digital format and making them available on the web opens them up for use by a much broader range of researchers, educators and students. For example, the Catholic University of America (CUA) Library hosts many historical scrapbooks and photo albums created by its alumni from the beginning of the twentieth century. The scrapbooks and albums are about 100 years old. Most of them are fragile, and some are in very bad condition. For this reason, they were stored in archival boxes rather than made accessible for browsing. After the collection was digitised, researchers and students were able to discover them and use them for a variety of unanticipated uses, such as for a film on the centennial of the CUA School of Arts and Sciences made by the Department of Media Studies (see the 'James Carroll Scrapbook' at: *http://www.aladin.wrlc.org/dl/collection/hdr?cuphoto*).

- *Improving discovery of individual items with online searching and browsing tools.* Creating appropriate metadata for digital images and documents allows digital collections to be searched and browsed by title, subject, personal name, places, date, and so on. For example, the *Treasure Chest of Fun and Fact* was a Catholic comic book published by George A. Pflaum of Dayton, Ohio. It was a bi-monthly publication from 1946 to 1972. The comic book contains stories that continued over several issues, even several years. Such serialised stories are brought together in the digital collection of the comic book, making it possible to view entire stories that were previously spread through different issues of the physical comic book. The digital collection also makes it easier to discover stories by the same author or illustrator (see *http://www.aladin.wrlc.org/dl/collection/hdr?treasure*).

- *Helping automate and simplify metadata creation and facilitating the cataloguing of large collections.* For example, the American University Library acquired a large collection of articles written by well-known columnist Drew Pearson in the mid-twentieth century. The collection contains over 20 archival boxes of original typescripts of Pearson's syndicated 'Washington Merry-Go-Round' column, published between 1932 and 1969. The typescript copies were sent to Pearson's office at the same time the typescripts were distributed to newspapers around the country. The documents had been in storage because the library did not have the resources to identify and catalogue the subject matter so that it could be used productively. When the collection was digitised, optical character recognition software was applied to create searchable PDF documents, allowing researchers to find relevant documents without extensive cataloguing and metadata creation (see *http://www.aladin.wrlc.org/dl/collection/hdr?pearson*).

- *Integrating related materials in various formats at multiple locations.* Items that cannot live together physically can do so online in a digital collection. Even if the digital content is distributed among a number of institutions, it can be aggregated online as a virtual collection. For example, the Collaborative Digitization Program (CDP), started in 1998 as the Colorado Digitization Project, is a collaborative digital initiative to provide access to the unique collections from archives, historical societies, libraries and museums in Colorado. For almost ten years, this statewide collaboration has integrated a vast amount of resources and a variety of formats that were physically located in many institutions to provide meaningful content on human culture, science and art to everyone connected online. While continuing to work with partners in Colorado and Wyoming, the CDP has expanded its efforts to collaborate with partners in ten western states, including Arizona, Kansas, Montana, Nebraska, Nevada, New Mexico, Texas and Utah (see *http://www.cdpheritage.org/cdp/history.html*).

These are a few general examples of value added by digitisation that should apply, more or less, to most digitisation projects. Other projects may have more specific benefits related to the unique research and education tools or methods available for the material, such as zooming and panning for high-resolution art images. Libraries should weigh the relative value added by digitising candidate content based on the project and organisational goals.

Target audience

When developing selection criteria for digitisation, libraries must be clear about the purpose of the digital collection – whether it be for preservation, outreach or curricular development. Libraries should clearly articulate which audiences are the primary targets for a digital collection. McDonald recommends defining a library's user community and selecting materials that are relevant to that community. He concludes: 'if we build high demand, high quality collections at a reasonable cost that can be maintained for the long term, we will take the first steps to becoming a major part of the scholarly research dissemination chain' (McDonald, 2003).

Clearly identifying the target audience will help develop effective selection criteria and save money and time by focusing on the relevant areas. For example, the International Children's Digital Library (2005) identifies two primary audiences. 'The first audience is children ages 3–13, as well as librarians, teachers, parents, and caregivers who work with children of these ages. The second audience is international scholars and researchers in the area of children's literature.' Therefore:

> the materials included in the collection reflect similarities and differences in cultures, societies, interests, and lifestyles of peoples around the world. The collection's focus is on identifying materials that help children to understand the world around them and the global society in which they live. (International Children's Digital Library 2005)

The material selection for the International Children's Digital Library would be different from selecting material for academic digital libraries, whose primary audience is faculty, scholars, researchers and students.

Technical feasibility

Technical feasibility is one of the most important criteria for selecting material for digitisation. The physical characteristics of source material and the project goals for capturing, presenting and storing the digital surrogates dictate the technical requirements. Libraries must evaluate those requirements for each project and determine whether they can be met with the resources available. If the existing staff, hardware and software resources cannot meet the requirements, then the project will need funding to upgrade equipment or hire an outside conversion agency. If these resources are not available, or if the technology does not exist to meet the requirements, then it is not technically feasible to digitise that material.

Considerations for technical feasibility include:

- *Image capture*. Image capture requires equipment, such as a scanner or a digital camera. Different types of material require different equipment, and different equipment produces images of differing quality. When selecting materials for digitising, technical questions that need to be addressed include: does the original source material require high resolution to capture? Are there any oversized items in the collection? Are there any bound volumes in the collection? What critical features of the source material must be captured in the digital product? In what condition are the source materials? Will they be damaged by the digitisation process?

- *Presentation*. Presentation refers to how the digitised materials will be displayed online. Consider the following questions to determine the technical feasibility of presenting the digitised material:

  - Will the materials display well digitally?
  - How will users use the digital versions?
  - How will users navigate within and among digital collections?
  - Do the institutionally supported platforms and networked environment have the capability for accessing the images and delivering them with reasonable speed to the target audience?
  - Do the images need to be restricted to a specified community?

– Do the images need special display features such as zooming, panning and page turning?

- *Description.* Some archival and special collections have been catalogued for public use and contain detailed finding aids with descriptions about each item and the collection as a whole. Other collections may not have been reviewed and documented in detail and do not have much information on individual items. Those collections will require more time, human resources and significant additional expense to research the materials, check the accuracy of the information obtained, and write appropriate descriptions to aid in discovery and use of the digital items. Typewritten documents, like the Drew Pearson columns described above, can have reasonably accurate OCR applied to them to replace, for some uses, the detailed descriptions required for discovery of hand-written or picture materials. The selection criteria should clearly state whether the items and collections that do not contain descriptions should be considered for digitisation.

- *Human resources.* When selecting materials for digitisation, the library should consider whether it has the staff and skill sets to support the digitisation, metadata entry, user interface design, programming and search engine configuration that is required for the project to implement the desired functionality. For large collaborative projects, dedicated staff are usually required from each partner. Digital collections also require long-term maintenance, which needs to be considered and planned for. If a project does not have the necessary staff and skills in-house, but funding is available, outsourcing may be a good choice.

Case study: DCPC's selection policy and service

The DCPC provides recommendations and technical advice for the member libraries to select appropriate collections for digitisation. Guidelines and requirements are developed to help the member libraries select their collections for digitisation.

The DCPC requires the owning library to affirm that it has the rights to digitise the material in the collection and disseminate the images. In cases where works to be digitised are covered by copyright, the owning library is responsible for obtaining permission from the copyright holder. A copy of the permissions document must be provided to DCPC along with the materials (Payne, 2004).

The DCPC encourages the member libraries to select collections that are permitted to be open to the public or, at least, to all libraries within the consortium. The member libraries may request assistance for collections that are restricted to one or more libraries due to the licensing agreement. The DCPC will provide services for such collection as time allows, but priority will be placed on the collections that benefit all member libraries within the consortium.

The DCPC Guidebook states:

> the DCPC is designed to support development of digital collections. The digital collection is not necessarily intended to completely replicate the archival collection – the most serious researchers will always need to work with the original materials. Rather, the digital collection is intended to provide online access to meaningful subsets of the archival collection, to promote awareness of the full archival collection, and, especially important, to bring archival materials to the attention of searchers who may not have known to search there. (Payne, 2004)

The DCPC provides advice on the factors that need to be considered when selecting for digitisation and guide the member libraries to identify values that will be added by digitisation. The libraries should consider the factors such as:

- Does the collection contain visual materials (photographs, graphics) that would make good use of online display?
- If the collection is largely text, would the content support and benefit from keyword searching, i.e. by OCR conversion or transcription?
- Does the collection complement other WRLC digital collections and expand the scope of a particular topic?
- Is the collection of a manageable size or can it be divided into meaningful sub-collections for online use? (Payne, 2004).

Technical feasibility is a major consideration for the DCPC staff to determine whether the digital conversion can be done in-house. As the DCPC has only two flatbed scanners that can scan material of up to 12 × 17 inches (30 × 43 cm) in size, we only accept materials that can fit in the capability, such as:

- non-bound materials such as photographs and letters;
- bound materials that can be laid flat on the flatbed scanner without damaging the binding;

- items smaller than 12 × 17 inches (30 × 43 cm);
- slides and negatives.

Another technical issue is metadata creation. Metadata creation is not only time-consuming but also requires knowledge of the archive or special collection. The DCPC is not staffed for creating detailed original metadata records. We ask the library if the collection has been processed sufficiently to include basic descriptive information about each item, or whether such information can be easily derived from the items themselves. If the metadata creation involves extensive efforts to research the original materials and detailed information, we will suggest the libraries outsource the project.

4

Metadata strategy

What is metadata?

'Metadata' means data about data. This simple definition implies that any structured information that describes the characteristics of a set of data is metadata. The term originally referred to descriptions of electronic data (i.e. produced by computer), such as a digital image, a word-processing document, a spreadsheet, an audio file, a website, and so forth. Any information about such computer-produced data, such as a filename, creation date, author, size, etc., is considered metadata. This term arose out of early efforts at describing, classifying and locating electronic resources. Now, however, the 'general understanding of metadata has since been broadened to include standardised descriptive information about all kinds of resources. This includes digital and non-digital resources alike' (El-Sherbini and Klim, 2004). Thus, a MARC (MAchine-Readable Cataloging) cataloguing record is metadata. An archival finding aid describing a collection is metadata, whether the collection is physical, digital or both. As Miller (1996) describes, 'One recognizable form of metadata is the card index catalog in a library; the information on that card is metadata about a book. Perhaps without knowing it, you use metadata in your work every day'.

When librarians create metadata for their physical collections they call it cataloguing. Metadata creation and cataloguing are two terms for the same activity (Caplan, 1995). Library professionals, specifically cataloguers, have been creating metadata for decades, recording descriptive information to manage and retrieve resources. Still, some confusion exists regarding traditional cataloguing concepts and practice and metadata creation. Some investigators have found substantial similarities between traditional library cataloguing practice and the creation of subject gateways. El-Sherbini and Klim (2004) conclude, 'In looking at this issue from the point of view of purpose or intent of metadata, one arrives at the inevitable conclusion that the differences are not substantial'. However, others argue that:

> metadata not only belong to a different production paradigm, but that they also are intended to be part of a usage context different than that of cataloguing records, and that they are technically linked to this context to a very high degree. (Gradmann, 1998)

We have found that although there are substantial similarities between traditional cataloguing practice and metadata creation, there are also significant differences that should be considered when describing digital collections.

Similarities include:

- Traditional cataloguing and metadata creation share a common purpose and intent – recording data for the inventory, management, discovery and locating of information resources.
- The descriptive elements (such as 'title' and 'author') recorded for an item, whether it is a physical or digital object, are very similar.
- Both rely on controlled vocabularies and cataloguing rules to ensure consistent description of resources.

Differences include:

- The digital object described by the metadata is often a surrogate of a physical item, and the original material may not be available for inspection.
- Metadata for digital resources is typically more granular than for physical items. Metadata records can be created at different levels. For example, metadata records might be created for each photograph in a digital photograph collection and for the collection as a whole. Metadata records might be created for a book and each chapter of the book. While traditional cataloguing deals primarily with one level of cataloguing for a book or for a collection, very few library catalogues contain records for individual photographs, book chapters or journal articles.
- Digital object metadata standards are usually designed to be simple and easy to create (e.g. Dublin Core, which is discussed below). Traditional cataloguing using Library of Congress cataloguing rules and MARC encoding is both rigid and complex. This implies that cataloguing physical items demands highly trained and skilled cataloguers, while digital content can be described by non-specialists and is more amenable to automated metadata creation.

- Certain kinds of metadata are specific to digital content, such as file format and object structure. This information is required for proper rendering of the digital object; a physical object, like a book, does not need to be rendered.

Roles of metadata

The key roles of metadata are:

- to enable content retrieval and rendering;
- to facilitate resource discovery;
- to ensure the integrity and authenticity of digital content;
- to document the intellectual and technical provenance of digital objects;
- to facilitate interoperability between diverse systems;
- to specify access and ownership rights and restrictions.

> There are many ways of categorising metadata, but one of the most common is to break it into three types – descriptive, administrative, and structural – based on the functions the metadata supports. These categories are used for convenience only – the boundaries between them are fuzzy and metadata often falls into more than one category. (Wendler, 1999)

Descriptive metadata

Descriptive metadata provides information about the intellectual content of a digital object. The most important element of descriptive metadata is a resource identifier that uniquely identifies the object. Other descriptive metadata elements include title, author, date of publication, subject, publisher and description. Descriptive elements support the discovery and locating of digital resources. Descriptive metadata is also used to document and track the intellectual provenance (e.g. origin, enhancement and annotation) of digital resources, which is very important for certain kinds of research collections.

Traditional cataloguing of physical collections is a process to create descriptive metadata. The library community has long been developing and using cataloguing standards and tools, such as AACR2 (Anglo-American Cataloguing Rules, Second Edition), MARC and LCSH

(Library of Congress Subject Headings). Truly, librarians invented descriptive metadata and this has been invaluable for finding information. Libraries have spent millions of dollars in creating descriptive metadata records for their collections.

Many cataloguing rules and standards that the library community developed can be applied to the creation of descriptive metadata. However, full compliance with traditional cataloguing rules is expensive and generally not necessary for digital collections. The ease of indexing and browsing digital content makes its discovery less reliant on detailed descriptive metadata.

Administrative metadata

Administrative metadata provides information to support management of the resource. Examples of administrative information include:

- technical information regarding the file's creation, format and use characteristics;
- information about copyright, licence and intellectual property rights;
- descriptive and administrative metadata regarding the original source from which a digital object derives;
- versions of the object;
- fixity information (e.g. checksums) for content files;
- the physical location of the original source and/or the digital object;
- the tools and equipment used to create the resource;
- the operator responsible for creating the digital file.

Administrative metadata plays a very important role in digital preservation by documenting the technical provenance of the content. This facilitates migration to new formats and moving the resources from one platform to another. With appropriate administrative metadata, one can easily identify the version and type of files, the name and version of the software used to create the files, and so on; this helps to understand and manipulate the content long after it was originally created. Administrative metadata can also help ensure the integrity of digital files, for example by recording checksums or some other kind of fixity metadata that can be periodically verified.

Administrative metadata facilitates both short-term and long-term management and processing of digital collections. Documenting the agents and methods used to create files and metadata will help narrow down the cause and responsible party if mistakes are found, and help to make the appropriate corrections. Encoding the rights for use that have been negotiated for digital content allows repositories and other systems to control access accordingly.

Structural metadata

Structural metadata is used to specify the relationships between components of a digital object (internal structure) and between different digital objects (external structure). This facilitates the navigation and presentation of digital resources by linking and sequencing related content, such as the pages of a document, chapters of a book, articles in a magazine, and so on (Kenney et al., 2002).

Internal structure is needed when a single item has component parts that are related in a specific way. For example, to turn pages in sequence for multi-page items, structural metadata must identify the first page image and list the sequence of the other images. To go to a specific section of a document and to view images for that section requires structural metadata to identify the page on which the section starts and the subsequent pages containing the section. Internal structural metadata is usually relatively 'flat', that is with only one or two levels of hierarchy, and fairly easily represented in an object's metadata.

External structure represents object-to-object relationships, such as the hierarchical structure of articles in an issue and issues in a volume of a serial publication. These structures can be much deeper, with many levels of hierarchy. External structure may also represent different kinds of non-hierarchical relationships, such as networks or webs. It is rarely practical to store the entire structure in each object's metadata. Instead, each object will have metadata describing its relationship to other objects, such as its parent and children (in a hierarchy) but not their ancestors and descendants.

Metadata standards

Careful design and creation of metadata facilitates the construction and utility of websites where the digital resources can be discovered and accessed. But this is a very limited way to disseminate the content. When researchers, scholars, students and other users discover useful content they invariably want to use it in new contexts, such as other websites, search engines, learning management systems and electronic publications. Good metadata is not sufficient for these purposes; what is required is good metadata that can be processed by diverse systems. For that, the metadata must be encoded in standardised schemas. As a result, many metadata standards have been developed and a great deal has been published about the various standards and schemas. Here we will introduce a few metadata initiatives that are most commonly employed in digital libraries.

Dublin Core

Dublin Core, the first 'metadata for the web' was developed in 1995 (Agnew, 2005). The goal of the Dublin Core initiative was to:

> define a set of data elements simple enough for authors and publishers to use in describing their own documents as they put them on the net, but useful enough to facilitate discovery and retrieval of these documents by others. This simple metadata could then also be used by catalogers and other third parties as a starting point for creating more rigorous or more detailed descriptions. (Caplan, 1995)

Their philosophy is based upon a minimal set of *core* metadata, enhanced by additional packages of metadata that are controlled and used by specific communities. General-purpose or cross-domain queries can be restricted to the core set, while digital collections of a particular subject area can make use of their community-specific metadata.

The Dublin Core Metadata Element Set defines 15 core metadata components, such as title, creator, subject, coverage and format. The core elements are applicable across a broad range of disciplines and projects for resource discovery and retrieval. Because of its simplicity and utility for a wide variety of resources, the digital library community has adopted it to describe electronic resources. However, Dublin Core does not include detailed administrative and technical information and it includes only one structural metadata element, so it is often supplemented with other schemas.

Dublin Core is an abstract model and does not define a specific encoding scheme. It is often expressed in an XML format such as Resource

Description Format (RDF). It can also be embedded in webpages by using the <meta> tag in the HTML header.

The Dublin Core Metadata Initiative (DCMI) is an organisation dedicated to promoting the widespread adoption of interoperable metadata standards and developing specialised metadata vocabularies for describing resources that enable more intelligent information discovery systems (see *http://dublincore.org*). The latest element set is version 1.1. Table 4.1 lists the 15 elements.

Dublin Core is now an international standard defined by National Information Standards Organization (NISO) Standard Z39.85-2007. The DCMI continues to promote the standard and help specific communities define 'application profiles' to describe their usage of qualified Dublin Core metadata (DCMI, 2006).

Table 4.1 Dublin Core Metadata Element Set, Version 1.1

Element name	Definition
contributor	An entity responsible for making contributions to the resource
coverage	The spatial or temporal topic of the resource, the spatial applicability of the resource, or the jurisdiction under which the resource is relevant
creator	An entity primarily responsible for making the resource
date	A point or period of time associated with an event in the lifecycle of the resource
description	An account of the resource
format	The file format, physical medium, or dimensions of the resource
identifier	An unambiguous reference to the resource within a given context
language	A language of the resource
publisher	An entity responsible for making the resource available
relation	A related resource
rights	Information about rights held in and over the resource
source	The resource from which the described resource is derived
subject	The topic of the resource
title	A name given to the resource
type	The nature or genre of the resource

METS

The Metadata Encoding and Transmission Standard (METS) is an XML-based encoding scheme for packaging descriptive, administrative and structural metadata regarding digital objects. The standard is maintained in the Network Development and MARC Standards Office of the Library of Congress, and is being developed as an initiative of the Digital Library Federation (see *http://www.loc.gov/standards/mets*).

METS provides a powerful means of combining all the elements of a digital object in one package. Rather than defining specific vocabularies for descriptive and administrative metadata, METS provides a mechanism for embedding other schemas, such as Dublin Core or MODS, in the METS package. It is also possible to point to metadata in external files.

A METS document can include up to seven major sections:

1. The *METS header* contains metadata about the METS document itself, such as the author or creator.

2. The optional *descriptive metadata section* is used for discovery and identification metadata. It can contain a metadata reference (a link to an external document) or a metadata wrapper or both. The wrapper packages descriptive metadata associated with the object, as either XML or Base64 encoded binary data.

3. The *administrative metadata section*, also optional, has four optional subsections for technical metadata, rights metadata, source metadata and digital provenance metadata. Each of these subsections, like the descriptive metadata, can include a metadata wrapper or reference.

4. The *file section* lists all the files containing content that makes up the digital object. Files can be grouped; some groupings might include master files, thumbnails, etc. The files may be referenced or wrapped internally as Base64 encoded binary data. This section is also optional, although most METS objects will include one.

5. The *structural map* is the only required section. It outlines the hierarchical structure and sequence of the digital object and associates the elements of that structure to the files and metadata pertaining to them.

6. The optional *structural links section* provides a means to link elements of the structural map to one another. This mechanism was designed to express the hyperlinks between webpages for digital objects that contain websites.

7. The optional *behaviour section* can be used to associate disseminators with content in the METS object. Behaviours include an interface specification and a reference to an executable service that implements and runs the dissemination.

The structural map, the real heart of the METS object, allows you to express the relationships between different expressions of the digital object (e.g. scanned page images and textual transcriptions of the content), as well as relationships between different parts of any given expression (e.g. the chapters of a book). The ability to package all the components of a digital object make it particularly suited for the import and export of digital objects between repositories. However, the optional aspects of METS can lead to very different implementations that hinder this kind of interoperability. To create and process interoperable METS objects, authors and programmers may follow a specific METS profile. Profiles for print material (books, etc.), photographs, musical scores and several other kinds of source material have been registered with the Library of Congress.

DIDL

The Digital Item Declaration Language (DIDL) is another XML package schema designed to represent the metadata, content and structure of complex digital objects. It was developed by the Moving Pictures Expert Group as part of MPEG-21, an open framework for multimedia applications (see *http://www.mpegif.org/resources.php#section42*). Like the METS schema, metadata and content files can be referenced or encoded (wrapped) inside the DIDL object. However, instead of separating different kinds of metadata, content and linkages into their own sections, DIDL uses a hierarchy of containers and items with elements to hold or reference metadata and content at each level.

DIDL data elements include *containers*, which contain *items* and/or other *containers*. *Items* contain *items* and/or *components*. A *component* contains a *resource* or *reference*. *Descriptors* contain attributes (metadata) associated with *containers*, *items* or *components*. A *resource* contains or points to binary data. A *reference* points to other elements in the hierarchy. DIDL *descriptors* are very powerful and flexible. They can be resource-based (containing a single *component*) or text-based (containing a single *statement*). The *statements* can contain any XML-based metadata schema.

This structure is simpler and more flexible than METS. However, implementers in the digital library domain have not developed profiles that would standardise usage of DIDL, so it is less suited for interoperability and more commonly used as an internal package format in repositories, such as aDORe at the Los Alamos National Laboratory (Bekaert et al., 2003).

Metadata strategy

Originally, metadata creation and maintenance was an exclusive domain of the library community. Metadata was primarily used to describe bibliographic material and relied on a single standard – MARC. Now metadata is used to describe a variety of material, from enterprise business data to hobby webpages. As a result, librarians are now faced with a wide variety of options for creating metadata to describe and share information resources. 'An organization developing a metadata strategy currently has many options: select an existing metadata standard, create a new standard, or blend multiple metadata formats into a hybrid standard' (Agnew, 2005).

When libraries first began digitising archival and special collections material, Dublin Core was an obvious choice for metadata. However, experience has shown that this simple descriptive schema is not sufficient for all the purposes and roles of metadata. Digitisation projects require a metadata strategy for selecting, designing and creating metadata. As Agnew (2005) points out, 'an organization developing a metadata strategy can create an empowering tool for its staff and its users, or make a very costly mistake that may require years for recovery'.

Identify metadata requirements

The first step in the development of a metadata strategy is to analyse the original materials and identify what kind of metadata is needed for discovery, indexing, display and retrieval of the digital objects. The considerations may include:

- *Characteristics of the original materials.* What kinds of material does the collection contain? Are there multi-page documents that require display tools to navigate? At what level do the materials need to have a metadata record? For instance, for serials, do you want to create metadata for each article or just for the entire issue? If you want to create metadata for each article, how do you connect the article and the issue together? If a collection contains photographs or other kinds of images, do you want to provide special viewing tools to support zooming or panning? Are there documents that require full-text searching capability?

- *Consistency in metadata from different institutions and across collections.* If the project is a collaborative effort, to what degree does the metadata have to be consistent? Is there a set of required metadata elements for all collections? Do you want to include metadata to identify sources, such as collection name and repository?

- *Presentation and navigation.* How do you want to display the metadata on the web? How do you want to index the metadata? How do you want to link different parts of the digital object?

- *Preservation and migration.* What kinds of technical information do you want to collect for preservation and future migration?

- *Staff and other resources.* Do you have trained metadata specialists in-house? If not, do you have funding to outsource metadata creation?

Select metadata standards

After the metadata requirements are identified, it will be relatively easy to determine whether to select a standardised metadata schema, develop a local metadata schema, or use a hybrid strategy. Consider not only the general metadata standards described above, but also specific standards that have been developed by various communities for material used in their domain or profession, such as the Content Standard for Digital Geospatial Metadata (CSDGM), the Metadata Standard for Electronic Theses and Dissertations (ETD-ms), or the Agricultural Metadata Element Set (AGMES). Standard schemas are preferred, not only for interoperability, but also because of the availability of 'crosswalks', that is, data element mapping tools that provide automatic translation of metadata from one schema to another.

Determine level of descriptions

The next step is to decide at what granularity metadata will describe items. What is the smallest unit that a digital object will represent? In a serial collection, for example, an object could be a page, an article, an issue or a volume. Describing each page individually does not usually have much benefit, while descriptions of articles provide access and discovery by title, author and subjects of each article rather than just a date or number for the entire issue. However, creating metadata at the article level requires significantly more staff time and effort, so one has to select a granularity that balances cost and utility.

Design descriptive and administrative metadata

Most metadata schemas provide some flexibility for implementation. Metadata design is the process of determining how the metadata schemas will be implemented, such as which elements are required, when and how to use controlled vocabularies, and what textual format to use for various elements. This design should be documented in a table or spreadsheet that lists each element, its attributes (e.g. qualifiers), usage (description of what information is recorded in that element), authority lists (if a controlled vocabulary is used), required/optional flag, and format (e.g. ISO 8601 for dates). This documentation will guide the metadata creation process and ensure that items are consistently described. It is also useful documentation for longer-term management and preservation activities.

Design structural metadata

Structural metadata requires special consideration during the design process, in part because there is no standard metadata schema that is designed expressly for all kinds of structural metadata. Packaging schemas like METS and DIDL provide a mechanism for describing the internal structure of a digital object. Descriptive schemas may provide a means for describing relationships to other objects (i.e. external structure), such as the Dublin Core *relation* element. Both kinds of structural metadata are necessary for the navigation and utility of digital objects. Structural metadata 'ties the components of a complex or compound resource together and makes the whole usable' (Wendler, 1999). For example, with complex documents (i.e. multi-page and/or multi-part objects) these uses include turning 'pages' (viewing subsequent or previous page images), navigating to a particular page or section, or switching views among available formats (e.g. page image versus textual transcription).

The following factors and conditions must be analysed and understood to design structural metadata successfully:

- *Understand the physical structure and characteristics of the original material.* The original material may have different physical structures. Some are single-image objects such as photographs, slides, art images, and so forth. Some are multi-image objects such as manuscripts, magazines and books. Some objects have a hierarchical structure, such as a book containing chapters which themselves contain articles. Some objects have both a horizontal and vertical structure. For example, a serial magazine may contain stories continuing in several issues, while each issue contains several continued stories. Some objects are related to other objects, such as a photograph showing a journalist interviewing an artist, an audio file of the interview and images of artwork being discussed. Each has its own metadata record to describe it, so the metadata for each object needs to reference the related items. Understanding the physical structure and characteristics of the material provides a foundation for the metadata design.

- *Understand the functionality and navigation requirements of the final product.* For example, the display page for an image object might list the metadata and a thumbnail or preview version of the image. When the thumbnail is clicked, a larger image might be displayed. For multi-page objects, the image display would need to include links to the next and previous pages and to jump to any page image. Hierarchical and relational material structures require additional navigation. For example, for a serial, a user may want to see the titles of each story, display an entire issue through a table of contents, or browse all pages in an issue from front to back. The user may also want to view a single story continued from issue to issue. For a scrapbook, a user may want to view pages in order for the entire book but also to zoom in or open up each item on a page. All of the necessary and desired navigation and display functions should be outlined when starting the metadata design process.

- *Understand system capability and configuration.* More than any other kind of metadata, structural metadata is highly interdependent with the systems used to publish and present digital collections. For example, as most digital collections are published on the web, links to internal components and other objects should take the form of a URL so web browsers can be used to navigate between them. If disseminator programs are used to provide special functionality, such as page turning or image zooming, then the structural metadata will need to conform to their requirements. Understanding the digital library presentation systems and disseminator tools will help design the most effective and useful structural metadata.

■ *Understand technical resources.* Creating structural metadata for very complex digital objects with many components can be difficult and error-prone. However, the process can be automated to some extent. For example, if filenames include page numbers then a script could automatically create URLs and sequence metadata. Tools like this are generally specific to particular ways of encoding structural metadata, so their availability should factor into the structural metadata design. In addition, consider whether and what kind of expertise is available in-house to create structural metadata creation tools.

Specify file naming convention

In most computer systems, names are used to identify files. As an identifier, then, filenames are an important piece of metadata. During digitisation, it is easy to simply make up names as you save each digital file. However, as the number of files increases this quickly breaks down; it becomes difficult to remember which files belong to which digital object or what parts of the object content they contain. Files should be named using a convention that identifies the digital object to which the file belongs and how it is related to other components of the object (e.g. sequence number).

A file naming convention should be established prior to capture. Filenames can either be non-descriptive or meaningful. Non-descriptive names arbitrarily assign an identifier to the object and component and are infinitely extensible (i.e. adaptable to any number and type of digital object). Meaningful filenames encode some descriptive information about object and component, such as format, page number, owner, etc. A file naming convention that uses meaningful names has some advantages:

■ It can be used to relate the digital content to the original physical item. For example, a filename 'b01f03-06' might indicate the original is the sixth item in Box 1, Folder 3. This will help staff members to locate the original material if it is requested by a user.

■ It can be used to specify structural metadata. For example, 'carroll-p23-A-02' might specify that this digital image is part 2 of item A on page 23 of a scrapbook named 'carroll'.

■ It can ease management of digital files before and when they are packaged into a digital object. Well-designed and meaningful filenames allow the staff members creating the digital content to identify files when looking at their names in a directory of folder listings. In addition, digital object creation tools can automatically determine how to put objects together when filenames are listed in the correct order.

■ It can assist in the automatic creation of metadata records. Meaningful filenames can encode descriptive metadata, such as date and volume and issue number, which digital object creation tools can then translate into standard metadata schemes and formats. However, care must be taken not to overburden filenames with too much semantic information that is difficult to encode and subject to change. Once the metadata record has been created, it, not the filename, should be maintained and used for discovery and identification purposes.

Creating meaningful filenames requires additional time and attention by the scanning technician, who assigns the filename to each digital image. The scanning technician must be trained to apply the file naming convention correctly and consistently. In general, the benefits of meaningful filenames outweigh these disadvantages for smaller-scale digitisation projects.

The software used for scanning may automatically generate non-descriptive filenames. Large-scale projects may use machine-generated names and rely on a database for associating each image with other images and metadata for the digital object.

When designing a meaningful file naming convention, the following rules should be considered:

■ The parts of the filename and any punctuation used to separate the parts should be consistent within a collection. Sequence numbers should always use zero-padding so that part of the filename always has the same number of characters. For example, an inconsistent file-naming convention might list sequential files thus:

– B02_f02-01.tif

– B02-f02-2.tif

– B02-f02_03.tif

However, a consistent naming convention would present these files as:

– B02-f02-01.tif

– B02-f02-02.tif

– B02-f02-03.tif

■ Define numeric parts of filenames carefully and avoid using long sequences of digits. For instance, because of the meaningless digits, using filenames like 'RG0031-001-0001-00002.tif' would likely result in a high rate of errors. Use the scope of each element of the file naming convention to determine the number of digits required. For example, if the archival box number is part of the name, determine how many boxes are in the collection. If there are fewer than 10, use one digit to specify the number. If more than 10 but fewer than 100, use two digits, and so on.

■ Take the sort order of your computer systems and scripting tools into consideration. For example, some systems will recognise that '2' comes before '12' while others will base the comparison on the first character only.

■ Do not include redundant information. For example, in most systems the extension already specifies the digital format, so it is not necessary to specify it in the file naming convention. Thus, the following names can refer to different formats of the same content:

– B01-f14-01.tif

– B01-f14-01.jpg

– B01-f14-01.pdf

– B01-f14-01.htm

However, digital format is not always equivalent to the different representations of the same content. For example, one might have three representations of each image: a master archival version, a medium-sized display version and a small thumbnail version. Some or all representations may use the same digital format and have the same extension, so the naming convention would have to specify:

– B01-f14-01master.tif

– B01-f14-01display.jpg

– B01-f14-01thumb.jpg

Digital object content model

The metadata design and file naming convention constitute a set of rules for creating digital objects. It is best to formalise these rules into models that define object structure and behaviour. Different types of digital content require different metadata and conventions, so a different content model should be developed for each type. For example, a finding aid might include an EAD document instead of or in addition to the Dublin

Core used for an image object. Once formalised, the content models can be applied to new digital collections to ensure that the tools developed for archiving and disseminating that type of object can be used.

The content model should include the following components:

- *metadata design*: the documentation of rules and controlled vocabularies described above, for each metadata schema used to record information about this type of object;
- *content file descriptions*: the kinds and formats of files, and the naming convention used for each kind;
- *internal structure*: how the content files relate to each other (e.g. sequenced, hierarchical);
- *external structure*: how the object relates to other objects (e.g. series, hierarchical);
- *disseminators*: what tools are used to view or play the digital object (e.g. page turner) and how the disseminators are invoked (i.e. a binding of the object components to the disseminator's parameters).

Case study: DCPC metadata strategies

As the DCPC only has a part-time metadata librarian, it was very important for us to select simple and standard metadata schemas and to automate the generation of metadata as much as possible. As described below, we devised several strategies to achieve this.

Strategy 1: use a single descriptive metadata standard

We selected qualified Dublin Core (Hillmann, 2005) as the metadata schema for descriptive metadata. Qualifiers are added when it is necessary to distinguish metadata that is refined beyond the Dublin Core elements. The qualifiers are created based on this recommendation from the Dublin Core Metadata Initiative:

> A client should be able to ignore any qualifier and use the information as if it were unqualified. While this may result in some loss of specificity, the remaining element value (without the qualifier) should continue to be generally correct and useful for discovery. (Hillmann, 2005)

For the most part, we select qualifiers from the application profiles that have been developed by DCMI working groups for library or digital collections material. Occasionally, no suitable qualifier is found in those profiles and we create a local one for our purposes.

We often receive metadata from our member libraries accompanying the materials to be digitised. The original metadata is in a variety of standard and unstructured formats, such as spreadsheets, word-processing documents, MARC records, commercial database records, and so forth. When possible we develop scripts that translate the information about the original materials to qualified Dublin Core.

Strategy 2: carefully design descriptive and administrative metadata

Metadata design is a critical process for the DCPC in creating digital collections. We design metadata based on the physical structure and characteristics of the original materials and the navigation and display functions that are required for the user interface. The metadata design process takes three steps. First, the original materials are carefully analysed. Second, the navigation and object display in the user interface are outlined. Finally, specific rules for entering or generating metadata are developed to support the functions that were outlined.

Our descriptive metadata is designed for consistency across collections. To assist with cross-collection searching and browsing, several elements are required to be entered in each metadata record, such as identifier, title, subject, type, repository, format and collection name. We also require controlled vocabularies for subjects. We rely on several controlled vocabulary resources: Library of Congress Subject Headings (*http://authorities.loc.gov/cgi-bin/Pwebrecon.cgi?DB=local&PAGE=First*), Thesaurus for Graphic Materials (see *http://lcweb2.loc.gov/pp/tgmiquery .html*), Art and Architecture Thesaurus (see *http://www.getty.edu/research/ conducting_research/vocabularies/aat*), and the Getty Thesaurus of Geographic Names (see *http://www.getty.edu/research/conducting_research/ vocabularies/tgn*).

Our administrative metadata is designed to record the scanning location and date, scanning resolution, bit-depth, compression and dimensions. These metadata elements do not generally display in the public interface, although box and folder information are often displayed as the 'material location', to aid library staff in handling requests and other management of the original material.

Strategy 3: design structural metadata according to established content models

Structural metadata design has been one of the most challenging tasks in our metadata design, as well as one of the most important. Many functions offered to the user depend on the navigational structure of the digital objects in the collections. For multi-page objects, to turn pages in sequence, structural metadata must identify the first page image and list the sequence of the other images. To go to a story in a comic book and view only the images related to this particular story requires structural metadata that identifies the starting page number and number of pages related to this story.

Informed by the use of a simple DIDL profile at the Los Alamos National Laboratory (Bekaert et al., 2003), we chose MPEG-21 DIDL for representing the internal structure of the digital objects. A DIDL document is associated with each digital object and includes information such as the sequence number for each content file, web-addressable links to each file, and links to related objects. It also describes the kinds of files that make up the digital object, distinguishing, for example, web display images, thumbnail images, master TIFF images, and transcription text files that may all be part of a single digital object. The Dublin Core 'relation' element is used to encode external structure. External structure represents object-to-object relationships, such as the hierarchical structure of articles in an issue and issues in a volume of a serial publication (Zhang and Gourley, 2003).

These rules have been described in content models for simple image objects (one display content file, no special disseminator, optional text transcription), complex image objects (multiple, sequenced content files, page-turner disseminator, optional text transcription), finding aids (EAD metadata, no manifest, XSLT disseminator), and others. Specific models for serials have been developed to relate issues and articles and allow browsing of either.

Strategy 4: design a meaningful file naming convention

The DCPC file naming conventions are usually based on the characteristics of the original material and functionality required to display the digital object. We design meaningful filenames that may include physical location of the original item, date of creation, hierarchy or sequences, and relationship of the items. Examples of such file naming conventions are:

- *Single page items stored in an archival box* – collection short name-box##-folder##-item##.file extension:

  Mitchell-B02F03-12.tif

  To avoid confusion and reduce errors, we try to include as few digits in the numbers as possible. For example, if the collection contains fewer than ten boxes, we would use a single-digit box number, for instance B1, B4, etc. The same goes for the folder and the item numbers.

- *Multiple-page items stored in an archival box* – collection short name-box##-folder##-item##-page##.file extension:

  Brooks-B03F13-02-01.tif

- Labelled items, such as slides and films – use the number on the original item:

  AT-01.tif

- *Magazines, newspapers, comic books, and other dated materials* – according to volume/issue/date/page extent, and so forth:

  vol01no02-03 – for volume 1, issue 2, page 3.

  b01f01-19321203 – for box 1, folder 2, 3 December 1932.

Strategy 5: create metadata efficiently using a all available resources and tools

Metadata creation is time-consuming and costly. As the DCPC is not staffed with a dedicated cataloguer, we try to automate the creation of metadata as much as we can. We will discuss how to create metadata records in detail in Chapter 6. Here we simply outline our approach:

- Create brief records with broad subject headings.
- Utilise the electronic files accompanying the materials, map the descriptions to Dublin Core elements and write a script to generate the Dublin Core elements automatically.
- Encode some metadata, particularly structural metadata, in filenames and write a script to create metadata based on the filenames.
- Use untrained staff to enter the basic identification metadata and let a trained cataloguer assign subject headings and other specialised metadata as needed.

- Use optical character recognition (OCR) on type-written text to create a transcription that can be indexed in lieu of subject metadata.

- Create templates for metadata entry that have fields already completely or partially filled in.

- Generate authority lists from metadata that has already been entered so the next time a value is used it can be selected from the list.

- Provide tools and instructions for the staff at the owning library to create metadata.

Designing metadata for the Treasure Chest of Fun and Fact Collection

Reviewing the original material

The *Treasure Chest of Fun and Fact* was a Catholic comic book published by George A. Pflaum of Dayton, Ohio, and provided to Catholic parochial school students between 1946 and 1972. The comic book was published twice a month. Each issue contained about ten stories. Some stories were serialised over several issues. Many stories were carried in many issues. One particular story started from the very first issue and continued for over 20 years. This comic book serial is organised originally by date, volume and issue.

Outlining requirements for display and navigation

As the title, subject and creator of each story provide more meaningful information and access points than the comic book title and the volume and issue numbers, we wanted to be able to browse and search the comic book by story/article title, subject and creator. We also wanted to display the comic book by each issue so that the user could browse entire issues from cover to cover. Serialised stories had to be linked together so that users could read entire series. In addition, each issue contained many activities and fun items, for example, 'arts and crafts', the 'puzzle and game page', 'how to...' sections and so forth. We wanted to group similar activities and items in categories so that users could find them in one place.

We outlined the display requirements as follows:

- browse by story title, subject and creator;
- browse by volume, issue and date;
- display table of contents for each issue;

- browse by series;
- search by keywords, title, subject, people, creator, series and date.

Designing metadata

The descriptive metadata is very straightforward and can be transcribed from each story and issue. We decided to assign a few simple subject headings for each story. The administrative metadata is also straightforward as we have designed standard administrative metadata for all our digital collections that includes image capture date, capture device and location, capture resolution, colour depth, compression, and so forth.

Designing the structural metadata was challenging. We decided to create a metadata record for each story, providing information about the title, author and/or illustrator and subjects. This would provide options for browsing and searching. To browse and display by each issue, we decided to create a record for each issue that contained only the date, issue title, and volume and issue numbers. Thus, each article record contains a metadata element 'DC.Relation.ispartof' to reference to the issue record, while each issue record contains a metadata element 'DC.Relation.haspart' to include all story records in this issue.

Figure 4.1 Structural metadata design for *Treasure Chest of Fun and Fact*

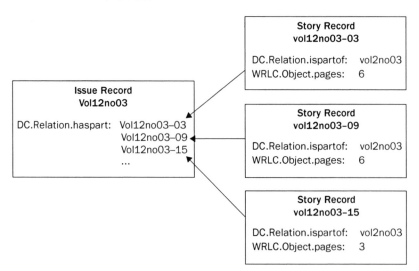

To link all stories in a single series, we used a metadata element 'DC.Relation.ispartofseries' to include the title of the series. We also used this metadata element to group the activity and fun pages.

The filename convention was designed to include the volume and issue number, as well as the page numbers. For example:

vol14no06-15
vol14no06-16
vol14no06-17

We designed a local metadata element 'WRLC.Object.pages' to input the number of pages associated with each story. When a story record is opened, only the associated images are displayed. Tables of contents are generated from the structural metadata. Figure 4.1 illustrates the structural metadata design.

5

Digitising material

Digitisation is the process of converting original physical material from its analogue format (e.g. paper) to a digital representation (e.g. an image file) using a computer facility such as a scanner or digital camera. A digital image may represent a photograph, a drawing, a hand-written letter, a map, a page from a book, and so on. The digital image can be viewed on a computer display and can be transferred over the internet to any connected computers in the world.

A large number of articles and tutorials have been written regarding the technical details of the digitisation process for images. The most popular publication is 'Moving theory into practice: digital imaging tutorial' (Kenney et al., 2000). This tutorial includes fundamental information on the use of digital imaging technology to digitise cultural heritage materials. It is intended to be used with another publication, *Moving Theory into Practice: Digital Imaging for Libraries and Archives* (Kenney and Rieger, 2002), which provides more details and advocates an integrated approach to digital imaging programs. Over 50 international experts contributed to the intellectual content of this book.

Another good online publication is 'Western States digital imaging best practices' by the Western States Digital Standards Group (2003). It outlines baseline digital imaging specifications for text, photographs, maps and graphic materials, and for quality control.

The 'Technical guidelines for digitizing archival materials for electronic access: creation of production master files – raster images' by the US National Archives and Records Administration (NARA) (2004) provide a complete overview of digitisation issues for textual documents, photographs, maps/drawings and other graphic materials. This very comprehensive publication covers metadata, workflow issues, digitisation specifications, storage and quality control.

'A few scanning tips' by Wayne Fulton (1997) offers extensive scanning tips and hints, fundamentals and other general scanning information. Although the site is not library-related, it offers easy-to-understand concepts and tips to help beginners get off to a quick start with their flatbed scanners.

SilverFast: The Official Guide by Taz Tally (2003) explains scanner technology and scanning basics in layman's terms. Although designed as a guide for using the SilverFast scanning software, it also provides superb information about basic scanning concepts in easy-to-understand language.

As so many good books and websites have already covered the details of digital imaging, in this chapter we will simply review basic concepts and highlight the most important aspects of digitisation.

Basic concepts for scanning

There are several distinct scanning factors that affect image quality. Understanding basic scanning concepts is very important for achieving the quality desired in the final result. Resolution, bit depth, compression, file formats and size, and so on, are the kinds of concepts to understand in order to convert physical material to digital images.

Resolution

Image resolution describes the image's level of detail – higher resolution means more image detail. In digital imaging, the resolution is often measured as a pixel count. A pixel (short for picture element) is a single point or a tiny square in a graphic image stored in an ordered rectangular grid. It is the smallest element in a digital image. The more pixels used to represent an image, the closer the result can resemble the analogue original. Figure 5.1 shows an icon that is enlarged seven times so the individual pixels can be clearly seen.

The resolution pixel count measurement is quantified for a specific unit of length. In the USA this unit is usually an inch and the measurement is called 'pixels per inch' (ppi) or 'dots per inch' (dpi), although dpi more accurately refers to the resolution of printing devices. When describing the resolution of a scanner or digital camera, ppi is the same as 'samples per inch'. The measurement describes the number of samples or pixels both horizontally and vertically in each square inch scanned. For example, 100 ppi means 100 pixels per inch, or 10,000 pixels in a square inch, and 300 ppi means 300 pixels per inch, i.e. three times the detail of 100 ppi. Figure 5.2 shows the same image scanned at different resolution.

Figure 5.1 Pixels in an icon

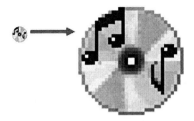

For many people, the term 'resolution' has been one of the most confusing areas of digital imaging. There is more than one kind of resolution and people tend to misuse terminology. Although ppi and dpi are sometimes used interchangeably, dpi has a distinct meaning when used to measure a printer's resolution. When viewing a digital image from a computer, the quality of viewing is affected by the screen resolution. An easy way to clarify the confusion is to make the distinction between *input* resolution and *output* resolution. Capturing an image using a scanner or a digital camera would represent input resolution. Printing or viewing an image would involve output resolution.

Documentation for different scanner programs may use different terminologies to describe input resolutions. For example, the SilverFast user guide uses dpi to refer to pixels per inch, so a 300 dpi scan will result in the creation of a digital image with 300 pixels per inch. The guide uses printing lines per inch (lpi) and a quality factor to determine the final input resolution. So an lpi of 150 and a quality factor of 2 will yield a final scanned image resolution of 150 lpi × 2 = 300 ppi (Hinderliter, 2003). It is very important to understand the specific

Figure 5.2 Same image scanned at different resolution

72 dpi   200 dpi   600 dpi

terminology that documentation uses in order to achieve the desired resolution.

Bit depth

Another important characteristic of a pixel-based image is its bit depth. Bit depth refers to the amount of information (stored as bits) that is represented by a single pixel. Understanding bit depth is also key to understanding the scan types or modes offered by many scanners.

All digital data, including image data, is composed of *bits*, which are pieces of information with only two values: 0 and 1. The number of bits used to define each pixel in a digital image determines the bit depth. Every pixel sampled is assigned a value that corresponds to the colour/shade it represents. The more bits per pixel, the more information can be represented and the more colours are available. Therefore, a higher bit depth can represent a greater number of colours or shades of grey. The capture bit depth describes the number of bits of image data that will be captured by a scanner or digital camera. For example, the bit depth of a black-and-white image is 1 bit, representing two tones, using the values 0 for black and 1 for white, or vice versa.

For digital colour images, each pixel is created through some combination of three primary colours: red, green and blue (RGB). Each primary colour is often referred to as a 'colour channel' and can have a range of intensity values specified by its bit depth. The bit depth for each primary colour is termed the 'bits per channel'. The total bit depth, referred to as the 'bits per pixel' (bpp), is the sum of the bits in all three colour channels and represents the total colours available at each pixel.

A common colour bit depth of 24 means the colour images have 8 bits per channel for 2^8 (i.e. 256) different values, translating into 256 different intensities for each primary colour. When all three primary colours are combined at each pixel, this allows for as many as $2^{8 \times 3}$ or 16,777,216 different colours, often called 'true colour'. This is referred to as 24 bits per pixel, as each pixel is composed of three 8-bit colour channels.

Table 5.1 illustrates different image types in terms of bit depth (bits per pixel) and the total colours available at that depth.

Increasing the bit depth enables the capture of more details, and therefore results in better quality, but will also affect resolution requirements, file size and compression. Reducing bit depth will result in smaller file sizes but somewhat poorer quality. Figure 5.3 shows how the quality degrades when a 24-bit image is reduced to an 8-bit image.

Table 5.1 Bit depth and number of colours

Bit depth	Number of colours available
1	2
2	4
4	16
8	256
16	65,536
24	16,777,216
48	281 trillion

Figure 5.3 Examples of different bit depths

The 24-bit image on the left is reduced to an 8-bit GIF image

There are three common types of digital images with the three colour modes as described below:

- *1-bit bitonal* or *black-and-white image.* This contains only one layer of pixels, with one bit of data per pixel. Each pixel can present two tones, which is either black or white. This is also called a line-art image.

- *8-bit greyscale image.* This contains only one layer of 8-bit pixels, each of which has the capacity to store and display 256 shades of grey.

- *24-bit RGB colour image.* This contains three channels of 8-bit greyscale pixels, one for each colour (red, green and blue). Each colour can be shown in 256 shades, so the total number of colours possible is 256 red × 256 green × 256 blue = 16.7 million.

Figure 5.4 Examples of different colour modes

1-bit line-art image   8-bit greyscale image   24-bit colour image

The images in Figure 5.4 represent the same picture scanned as 1-bit line-art, 8-bit greyscale and 24-bit colour.

Both greyscale and line-art images are commonly used to reproduce black-and-white images, but the greyscale mode is appropriate for photographs and anything else with a range of tonal values, whereas line-art mode is used mainly for reproduction of drawings or other high-contrast artwork and text.

Compression

Compression is the reduction of image file size for processing, storage and transmission. Compressed files are significantly smaller than their uncompressed counterparts, but the quality of the image may be affected by the compression technique used and the level of compression applied.

There are two types of compression:

- *Lossless* compression ensures that all image information is preserved, by removing only repetitive information. If the image is decompressed later, it would perfectly match the original uncompressed file. This is a process that reduces the storage space needed for an image file without loss of data.

- *Lossy* compression creates file sizes that are significantly smaller but it loses information in the process, by replacing data with resampled or predictive codes. When a compressed image is decompressed, it is no longer identical to the original image. Repeatedly compressing and decompressing a file with lossy techniques will cause it to progressively lose more quality.

To ensure that compressed data can be decompressed and viewed at any time it is important to employ a compression technique that is supported by standards, is non-proprietary, and is maintained over time.

File formats

Image file formats provide a standardised method of organising and storing image data in files. Digital image filenames generally include a graphic file extension that identifies the imaging standard that was followed in creating the digital image (Zhang, 1996). This filename extension designates the format of the file, for example, *.tif* for TIFF format, *.jpg* for JPEG format, and *.pdf* for PDF document.

Common standard graphic file formats used for digital collections are described below.

TIFF

TIFF (Tagged Image File Format) is one of the most popular and flexible of the current public domain file formats. It is a container format for storing all kinds of images. It can handle multiple images and data in a single file through the inclusion of 'tags' in the file header. It allows for a wide range of different compression schemes and colour spaces. TIFF is primarily designed for the interchange of raster data (i.e. pixel-based images). Its main strengths are a highly flexible and platform-independent format that is supported by numerous image-processing applications.

Image data in a TIFF can use lossy or lossless compression or no compression at all. The ability to store image data in a lossless format makes TIFF useful for archiving images. However, the image format is not widely supported by web browsers. In addition, uncompressed TIFFs are generally very large, and therefore not good for delivering and distributing over the internet.

TIFF filenames use *.tif* or *.tiff* extensions.

GIF

GIF (Graphics Interchange Format) is one of the two most common file formats for graphic images on the web (the other is the JPEG, described below). CompuServe, the first major commercial online service in the USA, commercially developed GIF in 1987. It was designed particularly for the 8-bit video boards that were common in PCs at the time. GIF uses a colour palette that is limited to 256 colours and is not suitable for today's 24-bit photo images. The images are compressed using LZW compression, reducing the file size by 30–50 per cent or more. GIF still works well for images that have fewer colours, such as line drawings, lettering, logos, bullets and icons.

GIF optionally offers transparent backgrounds, where one palette colour is declared transparent, so that the background can show through it. Interlacing is an option that shows the entire image initially at a low resolution with the image sharpening as the file download completes, which is an important usability feature with lower-bandwidth web connections. It also supports animations and allows a separate palette of 256 colours for each frame. These options make the image files larger.

A GIF filename uses a *.gif* extension. All graphical browsers and most imaging software support GIF format.

PNG

PNG (Portable Network Graphics) was designed to replace the older and simpler GIF format and, to some extent, the more complex TIFF format. PNG supports up to 48-bit true colour or 16-bit greyscale and uses lossless compression. Saving, restoring and resaving an image will not degrade its quality. This makes PNG a useful format for the storage of intermediate stages of image editing and enhancement.

A PNG file uses a *.png* extension. It is supported by all the major web browsers.

JPEG

JPEG stands for Joint Photographic Experts Group, the original name of the committee that wrote the image format standard. JPEG is designed for compressing either full-colour or greyscale images of natural, real-world scenes. It works well on photographs, naturalistic artwork and similar material. Its compression tends to blur high contrast images such as lettering, simple cartoons or line drawings (Lane, 1995).

JPEG uses a lossy compression method, which can reduce image file sizes to as little as 5 per cent of their original size. Though the amount of compression depends upon the original image, ratios of 10:1 to 20:1 typically cause very little noticeable loss of quality when viewed on a computer display. When a JPEG file is created or an image is converted from another format to JPEG, the user must specify the desired quality of the image. If the user chooses to create the highest quality image possible, the file size will still be relatively large. If the user is willing to sacrifice more image quality, the resulting JPEG file can be much smaller.

JPEG is one of the most popular image formats used for storing and transmitting images on the web as the differences between a minimally compressed and a more highly compressed JPEG image are not noticeable, while the file size is considerably different. This is due to the extremely effective compression offered by the JPEG file format, which enables people to quickly transmit (send or receive) image files over the internet.

Commonly used file extensions for JPEG files are *.jpg*, *.jpeg* and *.jpe*. The JPEG format is supported by almost all web browsers and imaging programs.

JPEG 2000

JPEG 2000 was created by the Joint Photographic Experts Group committee in the year 2000 with the intention of superseding their original JPEG standard. JPEG 2000 is the latest standard for still image compression, developed with a goal to achieve higher compression efficiency and error resilience. JPEG 2000 is a very flexible standard that allows the user to extract, from a single compressed file, various versions of the image with respect to resolution, quality and colour space.

Several advantages of JPEG 2000 have been claimed. It has superior compression performance over the original JPEG. JPEG 2000 decomposes the image into a multiple resolution representation in the course of its compression process. JPEG 2000 provides progressive transmission by pixel and resolution accuracy. This way, after a smaller part of the whole file has been received, the viewer can see a lower-quality version of the final picture. The quality then improves progressively as more data bits are downloaded from the source. The JPEG 2000 standard provides both lossless and lossy compression methods in a single compression architecture and makes it possible to store different parts of the same picture using different qualities.

JPEG 2000 file formats allow the storing of colour-space information and other metadata in the image, so the metadata can be transported with the image. This supports interactivity in networked viewing applications such as zooming features to see part of the image in greater detail. JPEG 2000 also supports transparent backgrounds. However, many web browsers do not currently support JPEG 2000. To view JPEG 2000 images in most browsers requires a plug-in. JPEG 2000 image files use extensions *.jp2* and *.jpx*.

PDF

The Portable Document Format (PDF) is the file format created by Adobe Systems in 1993 for document exchange. PDF is used for representing two-dimensional documents in a device-independent and display resolution-independent fixed-layout document format.

PDF is an open format developed by Adobe Systems as a standard for more secure, dependable electronic information exchange. It is recognised by industries and governments around the world. PDF is viewable and printable on any platform and many mobile platforms. Unlike HTML documents, PDF files display and print the same on a wide variety of devices and software platforms. They preserve source file information, including text, drawings, three-dimensions, full-colour graphics and photographs, regardless of the application used to create them.

PDF documents can be created as searchable PDFs, which leverage full-text search features to locate words, bookmarks and data fields in documents. Unlike a graphic image format such as GIF, JPEG and PNG, a PDF can contain multiple pages that can be enlarged to view details. The format supports page rotation, internal document links and bookmarks for different document sections, and links to external websites.

A PDF reader is required to view PDF documents. Adobe Systems provides a free PDF reader that can be used as a standalone program or a browser plug-in. A PDF filename has a *.pdf* extension.

File size

As discussed previously, a digital image is a rectangular grid of pixels. The image file data is organised according to rows and columns. By convention, image dimensions are written as width × height. For example, a 600 × 400 image consists of 600 columns and 400 rows of pixels, for a total of 600 × 400 = 240,000 pixels.

A greyscale image pixel typically consists of 8 bits, which is one byte. For a true-colour image, each pixel consists of 24 bits, which is 3 bytes – one byte each for red, green and blue. The image file size is calculated by multiplying the total number of pixels by the bit depth to determine the number of bits. Because the image file size is represented in bytes, which are made up of 8 bits, this figure should be divided by 8, thus:

file size = (width pixels × height pixels × bit depth)/8

For example, if the 600 × 400 pixel image is a 24-bit colour image, the file size is:

(600 × 400 × 24)/8 = 720,000 bytes

To bring those numbers into units that are more easily understood, divide the file size in bytes by 1,024 to get the size in kilobytes (KB), then by 1,024 again for the size in megabytes (MB):

720,000 bytes/1,024 = 703.125 KB
703.125 KB/1,024 = 0.69 MB

If we know the size of the original material in inches, and the ppi we are going to scan, we can calculate the final file size for the scanned image by the following formula:

file size = [(width × ppi) × (height × ppi) × bit depth]/8

For example, if we want to scan a 6 × 4-inch photograph at 300 ppi in true 24-bit colour, the file size would be:

[(6 × 300) × (4 × 300) × 24]/8 = 6,480,000 bytes = 6.18 MB

Because digital images often result in large files, the number of bytes is usually represented in increments of 1,024 or more:

- 1 kilobyte (KB)   = 1,024 bytes
- 1 megabyte (MB)   = 1,024 KB
- 1 gigabyte (GB)   = 1,024 MB
- 1 terabyte (TB)   = 1,024 GB

We can also calculate the scanning resolution needed to achieve desired file dimensions for different kinds of materials. For example, if the desired dimension for photographic material is 1,800 pixels across the long side, to scan a 6 × 4-inch photograph, we would need to scan it at a ppi equal to:

1,800 pixels/6 inches = 300 ppi

The University of Illinois Library has developed an online image quality calculator to help determine the recommended resolution for scanning documents and visual materials (see *http://images.library.uiuc.edu/ projects/ calculator*). Based on the information about the original material that is entered into the calculator, the program calculates the resolution in dots per inch (dpi), and indicates both the file size (in megabytes) and the pixel dimensions of the resulting uncompressed image file.

Master files and derivatives

Master files are used for archiving, for producing derivative files for different purposes, and for migrating to new formats in the future. Digitising the original material using a scanner or a digital camera creates master files. These are also called 'scanned files'. To avoid expensive re-scanning in the future when new technology emerges, it is crucial to scan the master files at the best possible quality and save the master files in an appropriate format.

Master files should meet the following requirements.

- scan at the best possible quality – scan once and use many times;
- file format must be standard, non-proprietary and platform-independent;
- file format must be supported by a wide variety of applications and operating systems for viewing, copying, editing, managing and transmitting;
- files must be saved in a lossless format;
- image quality must be sufficient for printing and publishing;
- file format should have the capability to hold metadata associated with the image, such as date scanned, technical specification, copyright information, and so on. The data will then move with the image, making retrieval easier.

The TIFF format meets all of the requirements and is recommended as best practice for the master file format. 'TIFF is the format of choice for archiving important images. TIFF is the leading commercial and professional image standard. TIFF is the most universal and most widely supported format across all platforms, Mac, Windows, Unix' (Fulton, 1997).

Derivative files are converted from the master files for displaying on the web and creating complex digital objects. Some of the characteristics of derivative files intended for displaying on the web include:

- standard file format that can be viewed from major web browsers;
- small file size that can be transmitted quickly over the internet;
- good viewing quality;
- searchable if there is significant text content;
- can be converted from the master files using a range of commercially produced and widely available software.

There are several format choices for creating derivative files, depending on the image characteristics and intended purposes. JPEG performs best on photographs and paintings of realistic scenes with smooth variations of colour and tone. PNG and GIF are good for charts, line drawings and other iconic or textual graphics. PNG can be used to store images in a lossless format, but the relatively large size of PNG files makes the format less suitable for transmitting over the internet. As GIF has only eight bits per pixel, it is not well suited for colour images. PDF is widely used for documents as it offers the ability to search the full text of the document.

As you cannot zoom in to view the detail in the most common display formats such as JPEG, PNG and GIF, they are not appropriate display formats for large-format images, such as maps, artworks, and the like. Some less common formats such as JPEG 2000 (*see http://www.jpeg .org/jpeg2000/index.html*) and MrSid (*see http://en.wikipedia.org/ wiki/MrSID*) are used for displaying large-format images. These formats use wavelet-based image compression, which is especially well-suited for the efficient transmission of very large images. For example, The Library of Congress uses MrSid to deliver maps from its collections. Both JPEG 2000 and MrSid provide zooming feature so that images can be enlarged to see details. However, major web browsers, such as Internet Explorer, Mozilla Firefox and Netscape, do not by default support the JPEG 2000 and MrSid formats, so the user will need to download and install a plug-in to view such images. Some commercial applications, on the other hand, do support JPEG 2000 and MrSid, as well as their zooming and panning features, without requiring a plug-in.

The Adobe Flash software is becoming more popular for developing special behaviours for digital objects. A Flash presentation can include animated and multimedia effects, such as page flipping, coordinated audio, animation and motion. Although a Flash plug-in is needed to view the Flash presentation, most web browsers are distributed with the Flash plug-in and users can view such digital objects without installing any special software.

Other file formats are also suitable for delivering images in different environments and you should consider which of these will be most appropriate for your project. Regardless of the specific formats used, it is best practice to keep three kinds of digital files for each image scanned: master file, display derivative and thumbnail derivative.

Scanning best practices

As original materials vary, scanning techniques also vary for different materials. Carefully reviewing the original materials to determine the best technique to capture the image is essential. User requirement is another factor to consider. For example, many aging papers have yellowish colour. Is it important to scan in colour in order to show the age of the paper? How important is it for the user to show the age of paper? These kinds of questions need to be answered before determining a scanning technique.

Testing and evaluating scanning samples before full production will ensure the quality of the scanning. One way to determine the appropriate scanning technique is to take a sample of the material, perhaps one with the greatest detail, and scan at a variety of resolutions. Using the medium with which they will be chiefly viewed in practice, show these scans to a sample of users and staff to identify which sampling rate best meets the needs for the digital object. This process will be most effective if you take into account the kinds of equipment your users will actually be using, for example, will they have access to high-end monitors and fast broadband connectivity? Once you have identified the optimum resolution then you can set the specifications for that collection.

Many institutions, especially those with large digital collections, have created guidelines for scanning and have published the guidelines on the web to document the best practices. The following list represents just a few widely adopted guidelines and best practices:

- 'California Digital Library best practices for image capture', February 2001 (*http://www.cdlib.org/inside/diglib/guidelines/bpgimages*);
- 'Library of Congress digital formats for content reproductions', July 1998 (*http://memory.loc.gov/ammem/formats.html*);
- 'NARA technical guidelines for digitizing archival materials for electronic access: creation of production master files – raster images', June 2004 (*http://www.archives.gov/preservation/technical/guidelines.html*);
- 'Western States digital imaging best practices', January 2003 (*http://www.bcr.org/cdp/best/digital-imaging-bp.pdf*).

Image processing

Image processing occurs after a digital image or scan is captured, and is a very important part of digitisation. Depending on the desired results, the process can be very time-consuming and expensive. However, this process may be underestimated and ignored, especially by institutions that are just starting to create digital collections. One of the authors encountered such situation in a collaborative digitisation project. The project proposal included only the cost for digitising photographs to master TIFF format but missed the cost of image processing, i.e. converting the TIFF files to display JPEG files. The project had to seek extra funding and resources, and reschedule time, later in the process, to complete the image processing.

Image processing may include the following tasks:

- *Enhancing images*: This includes steps such as cropping, touch-up, colour-adjustment, contrast adjustment, de-skewing (i.e. straightening out a crooked scan), and so on.

- *Creating derivative files or file format conversion*: This step converts the master files to display files and thumbnail files.

- *Scaling*: Scanned master files captured at high resolution will not be suitable for on-screen display and delivery on the web. Scaling, that is, resolution reduction through bit disposal, is often necessary in order to create images for web display and delivery.

- *OCR (optical character recognition)*: This step converts text in a scanned image to machine-readable text that can be indexed and searched.

- *Adding ownership statement*: This step adds a copyright or ownership statement to the lower border of each image.

- *Adding administrative metadata*: Information that helps describe, track, organise or maintain an image can also be added in the image.

- *Cleaning up scanned text for optimum OCR*: If the original material is in poor condition and the scanned text is not clean or sharp enough for OCR, it may be necessary to manually clean the scanned images to remove black dots and correct errors to achieve the best result. This process can be very time-consuming and expensive and therefore needs to be compared with the cost of manual transcription.

Many scanning programs can perform some image processing tasks such as automatic adjustment of brightness and colour, de-skewing, and edge sharpening. Good image editing software can provide easy-to-use tools for manual image processing tasks. Adobe Photoshop is one of the most widely used image processing applications. It supports a variety of file formats and conversions between formats. A handy Photoshop tool is the automated batch processing that provides a means to automate processing tasks that are duplicated for a batch of images.

Case study: DCPC's scanning service

Scanning materials to convert them to digital formats is a core DCPC service. Currently, the DCPC is equipped with two flatbed scanners that can scan materials up to 12 × 17 inches (30 × 43 cm) in size and a dedicated film scanner that can scan 35-mm films, negatives and slides. To date, the DCPC has been primarily involved with digitising photographic materials, archival documents, slides, negatives, and printed text that can be handled by the current equipment. We are not digitising maps, bound volumes, or audio and video at the present time.

To determine scanning specifications for individual projects, we always carefully evaluate currently available digital imaging technology and best practices. Following the general principles suggested by the Western States Digital Standards Group (2003), we scan materials at the highest resolution appropriate to the nature of the source material, scan at an appropriate level of quality to avoid rescanning and re-handling of the originals in the future, and create and store master image files that can be used to produce derivative files and serve a variety of current and future user needs. We have selected uncompressed TIFF as the master file format.

We also review and examine the source material to identify its characteristics for scanning requirements. If the original material is a type with which we have never previously worked, we perform thorough testing to determine scanning techniques. We select several typical items representing different kinds of materials in the collection, scan them at different resolutions and bit depths, print them out and view them on different monitors, and compare the results. We send the sample images to the owning library staff and ask them to review the sample images to make sure the scanning quality is sufficient for their requirements.

After the physical items are scanned and saved as master files, we process the digital images using a number of tools based on the characteristics of the material and the display requirements. Our image processing involves the tasks described below.

Add administrative metadata

We add some administrative metadata, such as collection name, keywords, scanning device, resolution, bit-depth and scanning location, to the master TIFF files. This process is completed using Adobe Photoshop's automated batch processing feature. The metadata is embedded in the TIFF files and can be viewed in Photoshop through the File/File Info menu.

Create derivative files

Derivative files are created from the master files based on material type and viewing requirements. In general, for materials such as photographs, handwritten materials, drawings, slides, postcards, and so on, we use JPEG as the display format. The conversion from TIFF to JPEG format is made through a batch process using Photoshop. In the same batch process, the file is scaled to 600 × 800 pixels to fit comfortably on most monitor displays. Usually some images are oriented as landscape (wider than tall) and others are portrait (taller than wide). To keep the original orientation, we identify and separate landscape and portrait images by putting them in different folders, then batch process the images using different parameters for each folder. In addition, in the same batch processing, an ownership statement is added to the bottom of each display image. The final JPEG images are saved at 'medium' compression level.

For text materials, such as printed documents, articles in magazines, typescripts and newsletters, if the condition is adequate for OCR, we convert the master files to searchable PDF for the display format. The conversion from TIFF to searchable PDF format is completed through a batch process using the Adobe Capture software.

Thumbnail images are also derived from the TIFF masters and completed using the Photoshop batch processing feature.

Enhance images

As we always perform testing to determine the best scanning techniques before starting a project and check quality during scanning, most of our images do not need to be cropped, de-skewed or re-touched. However, we occasionally receive images scanned by our member libraries and outsourcing vendors where the quality of the scan does not meet our standards and we have to enhance the images to improve the quality. This process is usually completed with Photoshop.

Split large PDF files

One interesting project involved a born-digital collection of journal articles that had been saved as PDFs. We received ten large PDF files from our member library, which contained 81 volumes of a journal. The 81 volumes included more than 430 articles and over 1,200 pages. The ten PDF files each contained about eight volumes of the journal and about 120 pages. Had we used the original PDF files for display, the download time to view them on the web would have been very long and finding the desired article would have been confusing for the user.

In this case, we used an application called 'A-PDF Split' to split the large PDF files into individual PDF files for each article. This process used bookmarks embedded in the original PDF files to point to the starting page for each article. The article titles along with the page numbers could then be saved as the filenames. We then created metadata records for each article using the filename and the page numbers. A locally developed Perl script automatically created the metadata from the filenames. After this processing, the final collection can now be browsed by article title, volume and issue number, and by date.

6

Creating metadata

Content rules for metadata creation

In Chapter 4, we discussed metadata standards or schemas. A metadata standard or schema is:

> a labeling, tagging or coding system used for recording cataloging information or structuring descriptive records. A metadata schema establishes and defines data elements and the rules governing the use of data elements to describe a resource. (Moving Image Collections, 2007)

However, a metadata schema does not specify how to determine the values or descriptions for the defined elements. In Dublin Core, for example, the element 'title' is defined as 'a name given to the resource'. (Dublin Core Metadata Initiative, 2006). It does not say where the name should come from, where to look for the name, and how to determine a title. If there is more than one possible name, which one should be used for the 'title'? If no name has been given to the resource, how do you (or should you) make one up?

As another example, consider the Dublin Core 'subject' element, which is defined as the 'topic' of the object being described. 'Typically, the topic will be represented using keywords, key phrases, or classification codes. Recommended best practice is to use a controlled vocabulary' (Dublin Core Metadata Initiative, 2006). The Dublin Core standard does not explain what a topic is, how to analyse subjects for a resource, or how to describe a topic or subject. It may be easy to find topics from text-based resources such as a website, an online article, or an e-book, but it will be difficult to analyse topics from a photograph or other pictorial works, as 'the delight and frustration of pictorial resources is that a picture can mean different things to different people. It will also mean different things to the same person at different times' (Shatford, 1986). A metadata schema does not address these issues. Knowing metadata standards alone cannot guarantee creating useful and consistent metadata; one must also understand content rules for determining metadata values.

Content rules or standards are the guidelines that prescribe what type of information is recorded in each metadata element, where to find the information (e.g. from a webpage header, a caption of a photograph, etc.), and how the information is formatted (e.g. should initial articles be dropped from titles, or should names be formatted as Lastname, Firstname, and so on). By using content rules, descriptions can be organised in a way that permits a high level of consistency and improved intellectual and physical access to the contents of any digital object. Standards also permit sharing of information with other institutions as well as within an organisation. Without using content rules or standards, a single element will be described in many different ways and each metadata record is likely to contain different kinds of information, leading to inconsistent metadata. Inconsistent metadata effectively hides desired records, resulting in uneven, unpredictable or incomplete search results (Hillmann, 2005).

The library community has well-established rules for data content. 'The Anglo-American Cataloging Rules', second edition (AACR2) was published in 1978. The rules were primarily intended for describing books, but over the years adaptations have been developed for graphic materials and archival collections. AACR2 is an internationally accepted standard for descriptive cataloguing. It is also a standard for structuring catalogues with headings and references to provide links between items with similar or related characteristics. The rules of AACR2 were written in a time when 'library catalogue' still meant 'card catalogue', but within a decade of its publication libraries were abandoning cards for electronic databases.

Resource Description and Access (RDA) is a standard effort to develop cataloguing rules to supersede AACR2. Work in this area has been taking place since 1997 with the International Conference on the Principles and Future Development of AACR. Initially, RDA was envisioned as a third edition of the Anglo-American Cataloging Rules, and was accordingly called AACR3, but in an effort to emphasise the break from the past it was renamed to Resource Description and Access. 'RDA is being developed as a new standard for resource description and access designed for the digital world' (Joint Steering Committee for Development of RDA, 2007). However, there is evidence that many individuals and organisations in the library community do not support this development of a 'next generation' of library cataloguing rules. For example, Coyle and Hillmann (2007) criticise the RDA as 'cataloging rules for the 20th century'.

The special collections and archives community has also developed standards for describing archival materials. In 2004, for example, The Society of American Archivists published 'Describing Archives: A Content Standard (DACS)':

> *DACS* guides archivists and catalogers in creating robust descriptive systems and descriptive records. *DACS* extends the skeletal rules for archival materials that comprise Chapter 4 of *AACR2*. It provides both specific rules for describing archives and illustrates how these rules might be implemented in MARC and EAD format. It includes crosswalks to these and other standards. (Society of American Archivists, 2004)

Standards vs. local decisions

Although several efforts have been taken place to develop or revise the traditional cataloguing rules to accommodate the needs for describing digital resources, nothing has been formally published and adopted for digital archival content. The traditional content rules, such as AACR2, consist of extremely detailed rules: pages and pages on how to determine the actual title of a book or how to arrange names in alphabetical order. Based on recent drafts, RDA does not appear to be any easier to use:

> RDA drafts reveal highly detailed rules with large numbers of special cases. The current plan for RDA contains 14 chapters and 4 appendices. Of the extant drafts, chapters 6 and 7 alone are 120 pages in length. It is hard to see how these rules can be anything but daunting, unnecessarily complex and expensive to implement. (Coyle and Hillmann, 2007)

When practical content rules are not available and the old rules are so rigid that they are not suitable for the digital collections, many libraries develop their own guidelines for creating metadata records based on their own collections and experience. The main goals of such guidelines are consistency and efficiency. That is, the libraries want to create consistent metadata records in less time and with less effort. The guidelines often include, for example, how to construct a title, how to input a date, how to input a place name, what controlled vocabularies to use for personal names, corporate names, place names and subjects, and so on. As subject analysis is very time-consuming and costly, some institutions decide not to do subject analysis for full-text resources, relying on keyword indexing to provide subject-based discovery of the objects.

Controlled vocabularies

Metadata defines the element set, that is, the pieces of metadata that will be used to describe content. Content rules suggest how to determine values for those elements. Controlled vocabularies are an important part of content rules that provide consistency in filling in the elements. A controlled vocabulary or an authority file is a limited set of consistently used and carefully defined words or phrases that have been pre-selected by the designers of the controlled vocabulary, in contrast to uncontrolled vocabularies where there is no restriction on the values that can be used. Controlled vocabularies enable librarians to provide uniform access to materials in library catalogues and to provide clear identification of authors and subject headings. For example, works about 'movies', 'motion pictures', 'cinema', and 'films' are all entered under the established subject heading 'motion pictures' (Library of Congress Authorities, 2008).

Conducting a search in a database that uses controlled vocabularies or indexing terms is more efficient and precise. Once a correct term is found, most of the relevant items are returned for a single search, meaning that there is no need to search for all the other synonyms for that term. Without basic terminology control, inconsistent or incorrect metadata can profoundly degrade the quality of search results. For example, without a controlled vocabulary, 'candy' and 'sweet' might be used to refer to the same concept. Controlled vocabularies may also reduce the likelihood of spelling errors when recording metadata (Hillmann, 2005).

The following are examples of some of the best-known controlled vocabularies:

- *The Library of Congress Subject Headings (LCSH)* comprise a thesaurus of subject headings, maintained by the US Library of Congress, for use in bibliographic records. LCSHs are applied to every item within a library's collection, and facilitate a user's access to items in the catalogue that pertain to similar subject matter (see *http://authorities.loc.gov*).

- *Library of Congress Name Authority File (LCNA)* contains 265,000 subject authority records, 5.3 million name authority records (ca. 3.8 million personal, 900,000 corporate, 120,000 meeting and 90,000 geographic names), 350,000 series and uniform title authority records, and 340,000 name/title authority records (see *http://authorities.loc.gov* and *http://authorities.loc.gov/help/contents.htm*).

- *Thesaurus for Graphic Materials (TGM)*, which was published in October 2007. TGM was the result of merging the Thesaurus of Graphic Materials I (TGM-I) and Thesaurus of Graphic Materials II (TGM-II) into a single vocabulary. TGM-I was compiled by the Prints and Photographs Division of Library of Congress, and consists of thousands of terms and numerous cross-references for the purpose of indexing visual materials. TGM-II, also compiled by the Library of Congress, is a thesaurus of more than 600 terms to describe genre and physical characteristic terms (see *http://lcWeb2.loc.gov/pp/tgmiquery.html*).

- *The Art and Architecture Thesaurus (AAT)*, developed and maintained by the Getty Museum, is a structured vocabulary of around 34,000 concepts, including 131,000 terms, descriptions, bibliographic citations, and other information relating to fine art, architecture, decorative arts, archival materials and material culture (see *http://www.getty.edu/research/conducting_research/vocabularies*).

- *The Getty Thesaurus of Geographic Names (TGN)* is a structured vocabulary containing around 912,000 records, including 1.1 million names, place types, coordinates and descriptive notes, focusing on places important for the study of art and architecture (see *http://www.getty.edu/research/conducting_research/vocabularies/tgn*).

Smith-Yoshimura (2007) reports that more than two-thirds of respondents use the Library of Congress Subject Headings, the Library of Congress Name Authority File, and the Art and Architecture Thesaurus in their descriptive metadata creation. Nevertheless, about half the respondents build and maintain one or more local thesauri.

Tools for metadata creation

A great variety of tools can be used for metadata creation. The tools vary with the data structure and data content standards being used, and, to some degree, with the types of materials being described.

Smith-Yoshimura (2007) reports that when 'asked to name all the tools used to create, edit, and store metadata descriptions, respondents listed a total of 263 tools'.

Examples of metadata creation tools for digital collections include the following:

- digital library software, such as CONTENTdm (*http://www.oclc.org/ contentdm/default.htm*), Greenstone Digital Library Software (*http://www.greenstone.org*), and Insight Software (*http://www .lunaimaging.com/insight/index.html*);

- institutional repository software, such as DSpace (*http://www.dspace .org*) and EPrints (*http://www.eprints.org*);

- archival management systems, such as Archivists' Toolkit (*http:// www.archiviststoolkit.org*) and Re:discovery (*http://www.rediscovery software.com*);

- integrated library systems, such as Ex Libris' ALEPH (*http://www .exlibrisgroup.com/aleph.htm*) or Voyager (*http://www.exlibrisgroup.com/ voyager.htm*), Innovative Interfaces' Millennium (*http://www.iii.com/ mill/index.shtml*), and SirsiDynix's Unicorn (*http://www.sirsidynix .com/Solutions/Products/integratedsystems.php*);

- desktop spreadsheet or database applications, such as Microsoft Excel or Access;

- word-processing software or text editors, such as Microsoft Word or Notepad;

- XML editors, such as Altova XMLSpy and SyncRO Soft oXygen.

In addition, there are many locally developed tools using, for example, web forms for entering metadata. Smith-Yoshimura reports:

> The single most common response was 'a customized tool', cited by 69% of all respondents. These include homegrown tools for creating, managing, or providing access to archival collections or finding aids, images, digital assets, and collection or content management. (Smith-Yoshimura, 2007)

Although there are many tools available for metadata creation, very few have all the features that make it easy and efficient to create consistent metadata records. These features include:

- *authority control*: to select predefined terms from a controlled vocabulary;

- *global replacement*: to make corrections in selected or all records in batch mode;
- *templates*: to set up default values for similar records;
- *batch metadata creation*: to import metadata from external sources in a variety of formats and schemas;
- *spell-check*: to flag and, perhaps, to fix spelling errors.

Computer-assisted metadata creation

Because the process of identifying and documenting metadata is so time-consuming, metadata creation tools should be used to automate the process to the extent possible. For example, we have mentioned how OCR can be used on images of typewritten text with sufficient accuracy to support keyword indexing to replace the laborious documentation of subject metadata. This does not provide the discovery benefits of a metadata element with a controlled vocabulary, but the OCR process can be automated and enable the digitisation of very large collections that would simply not be possible if every object was thoroughly analysed and catalogued by subject.

When entering specific subject metadata for each object, good metadata creation tools can partially automate the process. If a controlled vocabulary is not available, but many values, such as personal names, are used over and over, the tools can build up an authority list from the metadata that has been created. This allows the metadata technician to select the value from the list the next time it needs to be entered. This kind of authority list can also be used for error checking, as misspellings will almost always show up on the alphabetical list next to or near the correct entry.

Another way software tools can be used to assist in metadata creation is to decode information from filenames to generate properly formatted metadata and automatically create complex structured digital objects. In Chapter 4 we described how a meaningful file naming convention could be used to indicate which files belong in the same digital object and how they are related to other digital objects (e.g. articles related to the serial issue in which they were published). The file naming convention can also include other descriptive information that is easy to encode, such as publication date, document type, and so on. An intelligent metadata creation tool can be programmed to collect files for a digital object, structure them correctly based on a page or other sequence number in the name, and decode any other information that has been included in the filename. The resulting structured digital object can be manually enhanced with additional descriptive information much more easily than if all descriptive and structural metadata had to be entered to create the object.

For example, suppose a file naming scheme for articles in a serial publication is to name each page display image with names like *v01no02-03.jpg*, where the first number is the volume, the second the issue and the third the page. To create a digital object for an article, the data entry staff might browse the images and select the page on which the article starts. The metadata creation tool, if it had been programmed to parse the filename, could automatically create the volume, issue and page number metadata. If the data entry staff also specified the number of pages that the article spanned, the tool could create the digital object by collecting all the page images and packaging them with the metadata record. If the article in this example is three pages long, the object would automatically include the image files *v01no02-03.jpg*, *v01no02-04.jpg* and *v01no02-5.jpg*.

If any electronic information describing the physical resources, such as a finding aid or inventory list, is available, software tools can be used to create a batch of digital objects from the electronic data and the digital files. In this case, it is important to include some identifier from the data in the filenames. If the inventory list has an item or catalogue number, this can be used. In some finding aids, the only identifying information might be the physical location, such as box, folder and item sequence numbers. These can be combined to create an identifier that is unique within the collection. This allows the metadata creation tool to map the appropriate metadata to the digital files and create the digital object.

When creating batches of digital objects to import into a digital collection, the objects must be packaged in the format expected by the collection management or presentation system. While the content of these packages is typically standard metadata schemas and digital file formats, the way those components are packaged together varies from system to system. The schemas and formats used in the original electronic data are much more variable. The information in the collection may have been maintained in a PC database in an obsolete or non-standard schema. No tools are available to process all the various formats of electronic data that might be found describing archival collections. In many cases, a custom script will have to be written to read the data and create the digital objects packaged appropriately for the target system. Perl is an excellent scripting language for this kind of task because of its very powerful string processing and pattern matching features (see *http://www.perl.com*). Some custom programming effort will be required to create batches from each new data source, although this can be eased somewhat by creating a reusable module to do the digital object creation and packaging, as this will be the same as long as the batches are imported into the same collections management or presentation system.

Metadata crosswalk (data mapping)

Actually, the custom programming may be the easiest part of creating digital objects from existing electronic descriptions. The challenging part is often figuring out how to map the existing data to the target metadata schema. For translating between different metadata element sets, a metadata creation tool needs a precise specification, known as a metadata crosswalk.

If the digital collection system cannot handle a certain metadata schema, that type of metadata must be 'translated' to a metadata schema that the system can support. For example, existing library collections information has often been created using the MARC format, but most digital collections systems and metadata creation tools do not support MARC. Therefore the MARC records must be converted to something like Dublin Core, which is more commonly supported in digital libraries. The fields in MARC records are mapped to elements in Dublin Core that have the same or similar meanings.

The Library of Congress has developed several crosswalks (see *http://www.loc.gov/marc/marc2dc.html*). Table 6.1 presents an example of a MARC to Dublin Core crosswalk.

OCLC has developed a metadata crosswalk repository, called SchemaTrans (see *http://www.oclc.org/research/researchworks/schematrans/default.htm*). The repository improves the usability of the bibliographies by collecting all information required to document and execute a collection of crosswalks.

The following are some of the crosswalks that are freely available on the web:

- Dublin Core – MARC (see *http://www.loc.gov/marc/dccross.html* and *http://www.loc.gov/marc/marc2dc.html*);

- MARC – MODS (Metadata Object Description Schema) and Dublin Core – MODS (see *http://www.loc.gov/standards/mods/mods-conversions.html*);

- MARC – EAD (see *http://www.loc.gov/ead/tglib/appendix_a.html*).

Table 6.1   MARC to Dublin Core crosswalk

Dublin Core element	MARC fields
Title	245
Creator	100, 110, 111, 700, 710, 711, 720
Subject	600, 610, 611, 630, 650, 653
Description	500–599, except 506, 530, 540, 546
Contributor	
Publisher	260ab
Date	260$c
Type	Leader06, Leader07, 655
Format	856$q
Identifier	856$u
Source	786ot
Language	008/35–37, 546
Relation	530, 760–787ot
Coverage	651, 752
Rights	506, 540

There are also many non-standard metadata schemas created in various systems and databases. Some commercial databases use their own metadata schemas. In these cases there may be no established crosswalk to use and one may need to develop a crosswalk or data mapping system. It is not an easy task to map data from one metadata schema to another. The following are some of the issues to consider when creating a custom crosswalk:

- *Understand the original data.* The original data should be analysed carefully. It is very important to understand each field, not only by the element name or field tag but also by the various values that might be in those fields. In many cases, especially with databases created a long time ago, the terms or tags used by the original designer of the database or dataset may be very different from what we are using now. A designer with a computer background may design a database differently from a librarian. Understanding the content of the original data will help in mapping the data correctly to a new schema.

- *Understand the target metadata standard.* The metadata standard to which data are being mapped should also be studied and understood.

To create the correct mapping, study the metadata's definition, content rules and examples.

- *Understand target system requirements.* The collections management system being used needs to be analysed for its metadata requirements. For example, sometimes, a system may reserve specific metadata elements for system use, such as a date element for documenting when a digital object is accessioned into the system.

- *Preserve all data from the original metadata.* Even after all this analysis you may not find the target metadata element that exactly fits some of the original metadata. However, this original metadata should not be discarded. It should be put in a 'best fit' target metadata element or into a local extension to the target schema. The designer of the original database designed the metadata for a reason and it took time and money to create it; it costs very little to map and store the metadata for some future use that might not be understood today.

Case study: DCPC's metadata creation

The DCPC uses various methods and tools for metadata creation as our data comes from a variety of sources. Some collections come without any metadata and some are accompanied by brief information. Some archivists have created metadata in a unique format or using a custom database. Some libraries can employ student labour to create metadata for their new digital collections, and require the DCPC to provide detailed instructions for creating metadata in a consistent format.

Metadata practice

To create consistent metadata records for all digital collections in the consortium, we require each collection to contain at least the following metadata elements: identifier, title, type, repository, format and collection name. Subject should also be included unless the digital objects include text transcriptions that can be indexed.

If we need to create metadata records from scratch, we use the AACR2 rules as guidelines with some local modifications. For example, titles for correspondences are constructed in the following way:

Letter from [Sender] to [Recipient], [Date]

Thus:

> Letter from Humphrey O'Riordan to James O'Brien, April 22, 1880.

We also use controlled vocabularies for subject headings. We recommend three controlled vocabulary resources: Library of Congress Subject Headings (LCSH), Thesaurus for Graphic Materials (TGM), and Art and Architecture Thesaurus (AAT). For personal and corporate names, we use Library of Congress Name Authority File (LCNA). For place names, we use the Getty Thesaurus of Geographic Names (TGN).

The DCPC staff create metadata records using a template designed for a specific collection. In some cases, the owning libraries have staff and funding available for metadata creation. In such cases, the DCPC staff then design the metadata and provide instructions for the library staff to create metadata records using the DCPC's tools. A great number of metadata records are created in batch using Perl scripts written by WRLC IT staff to decode information in filenames. The DCPC also creates collection-level records for each digital collection and enters these records in the consortium's union library catalogue system, from which they are then contributed to the national bibliographic databases.

Tools for metadata creation

When the DCPC was first set up we adapted a tool called DC-dot that was developed at the University of Köln for describing HTML pages and embedding Dublin Core metadata in the HTML file (see *http://www .ukoln.ac.uk/metadata/dcdot*). This tool featured a simple and flexible web form for entering information and created an HTML file that was, at the time, a useful format for storing our metadata records. However, over time we added a number of custom features to DC-dot, such as templates and authority list drop-down menus, and disabled a number of DC-dot features that we were not using. When we added a fully functional repository to our digital collections management system (as described in the case study in Chapter 9) we decided to write a new metadata creation tool that we call DCEditor, which could be integrated with the new repository. We kept the easy-to-use web form interface and our local customisations, and changed the metadata record format from HTML to XML.

The current features of DCEditor include:

- *Digital object identification.* A list of digital files available for cataloguing is automatically generated with links to view the content. An object identifier can be specified to indicate which files are to be included in the object; those files with the identifier encoded in them are automatically structured according to their type and sort order. Once the digital object is created and submitted to the repository, the image files in that object are removed from the list.

- *Local authority control.* The data entry form includes drop-down pick lists for selecting standard metadata values, such as personal names, subjects, material types, and so on. Authority files can be created from standard vocabularies, or automatically generated from existing metadata in the collection. Data entry staff can pick authority values from the list, resulting in simpler data entry and fewer errors.

- *Metadata editing.* The editor allows searching, jumping to a record, editing and deleting records, adding new fields, and adding or replacing content files.

- *Template creation.* Templates for various kinds of records can be created and used to automatically generate metadata for Dublin Core fields.

- *Digital content access.* Master and derivative image files can be viewed and retrieved.

- *Batch metadata creation.* The tool allows for a record or batch record to be created automatically for images in a specified folder. A custom script can be written for each collection which is invoked to generate the records based on that collection's naming convention.

- *Web interface.* The editor has a web form interface that can be used by authorised staff both onsite and at remote locations.

As the DCPC is staffed with only a part-time metadata librarian, the DCEditor is designed to automatically generate as much metadata as possible. For example, magazine metadata, if not catalogued at the article level, is a good candidate for generating metadata from filenames and templates, because the title is the same for every issue and the dates and volume and issue numbers can be easily encoded in the filenames. Structural metadata relating magazine volumes and issues (and articles, if catalogued) is also encoded in filenames, which the DCEditor then uses to create Dublin Core 'relation' *ispartof* and *haspart* qualified metadata elements.

To handle the variety of formats in which we receive descriptive information for collections, we have developed a few Perl scripts to parse the input metadata and package digital objects in a form that can be imported into the repository. The scripts use a common module for creating the import packages. They also use simple Perl to include files to specify the crosswalk so that when we get another collection's metadata in that format, the original Perl script can be used by simply creating a new crosswalk. We have created scripts for metadata from ISIS databases, the Re:discovery system, and various other XML and delimited text file formats.

Creating records for the Drew Pearson's 'Washington Merry-Go-Round' Collection

The Drew Pearson's 'Washington Merry-Go-Round' Collection, from the American University Library Special Collections, contains the typescript copies of Pearson's syndicated 'Washington Merry-Go-Round' column, published between 1932 and 1969 (see *http://www.aladin.wrlc.org/dl/collection/hdr?pearson*). The physical collection contains 20 archival boxes of the typescript copies of the articles written by Drew Pearson every day, except Sundays, for more than 30 years. The collection came to DCPC without any metadata. As the material is mostly text, we decided to create searchable PDF documents for the typescript copies. The Greenstone software we used for indexing and presentation has a PDF plug-in that can extract the first line of a PDF document as a title to display. However, the quality of the typescripts was very poor and although the first line of the document varied, the title generally did not, making it impossible to use the Greenstone PDF utility to create metadata records. Creating the metadata manually was also not viable, as it would have taken our part-time metadata librarian a number of years to create the more than 15,000 records.

After carefully analysing the original material, we found the majority of articles had dates and consistent title categories. We could therefore design a good file naming structure and automatically create metadata from the filenames.

We designed filename convention as follows:

/year/box##folder##-(date)####item-pag##.extention

For example:

/1932/b01f01-1221-01.tif

/1932/b01f01-1221-02.tif

indicates:

Box 1, Folder 1, December 21, 1932, The Daily Washington Merry-Go-Round. The document contains two pages.

We identified eight categories of title and assigned a letter code to each category. For example,

- For 'The Weekly Washington Merry-Go-Round', put 'w' after the date:

/1933/b01f05-0806w-01.tif

represents page 1 of 'The Weekly Washington Merry-Go-Round', August 6, 1933, in Box 1, Folder 5.

- For the 'Washington Merry-Go-Round', put 'z' after the date:

/1934/b01f08-0913z-02.tif

indicates page 2 of 'Washington Merry-Go-Round', September 13, 1934, in Box 1, Folder 8.

- For 'To Washington Merry-Go-Round subscribers', put 's' after the date:

/1938/b03f05-0712s-01.tif

represents page 1 of 'To Washington Merry-Go-Round subscribers', July 12, 1938, in Box 3, Folder 5.

If a title cannot be identified, we assign a letter 'x'. If a date cannot be identified, we assign a letter 'u'.

Table 6.2 shows the code used in the filename for different titles.

The filenames and the code were assigned by the scanning technician during the scanning process. Eight metadata templates were created for the programmer to develop a script to automatically create metadata records based on the filenames. Each template represents a title category with related creator names and publisher. All templates contain several default values, such as resource type, digital format, language, collection name, rights and repository. Variables such as dates, number of pages, box and folder numbers, and date of creation are identified from the

Table 6.2 Codes for different titles

Code	Title
No code	The Daily Washington Merry-Go-Round
a	Editor's Note
b	Note to Editors
w	The Weekly Washington Merry-Go-Round
z	The Washington Merry-Go-Round
s	To Washington Merry-Go-Round subscribers
u	No date
x	No title

Figure 6.1 Example of creating a metadata record based on the filename

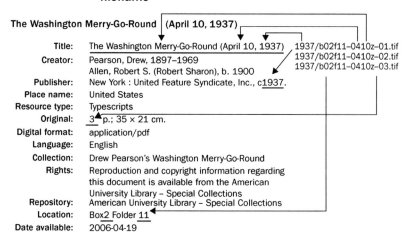

The Washington Merry-Go-Round (April 10, 1937)

Title:	The Washington Merry-Go-Round (April 10, 1937)
Creator:	Pearson, Drew, 1897–1969
	Allen, Robert S. (Robert Sharon), b. 1900
Publisher:	New York : United Feature Syndicate, Inc., c1937.
Place name:	United States
Resource type:	Typescripts
Original:	3 p.; 35 × 21 cm.
Digital format:	application/pdf
Language:	English
Collection:	Drew Pearson's Washington Merry-Go-Round
Rights:	Reproduction and copyright information regarding this document is available from the American University Library – Special Collections
Repository:	American University Library – Special Collections
Location:	Box2 Folder 11
Date available:	2006-04-19

1937/b02f11–0410z–01.tif
1937/b02f11–0410z–02.tif
1937/b02f11–0410z–03.tif

filename and are automatically inserted in the record. Figure 6.1 illustrates the process of creating the metadata records based on the filename. The underlined texts are variables decoded from the filenames.

This process is very fast. There are about 450 articles in each year and the records can be created in seconds. After the records are created, we do a search in the metadata editor to pull out those 'no title' and 'no date' records and edit them manually according to the actual title in the documents.

7

Designing a user interface for digital collections

The user interface is the way software presents its underlying functionality to the outside. The user interface acts as an intermediary between a computer program and the user. In other words, a user interface is a collection of techniques and mechanisms that allow the user to interact with the computer program.

A great deal of research has been conducted in user interface design. User interface design is a major job for software designers. The digital collection system you purchased or selected already has user interfaces for staff users and for general public users. The aim of user interface design for digital collections is to maximise the power and capability of the system interface to present the collection's digital content according to organisational requirements and user needs.

Most digital collection systems allow end users to configure the interfaces, including the staff user interface and public user interface. Some digital library systems only allow limited customisation, such as changing colours, adding links to local websites, changing logo and header graphics, and so on. Other systems, meanwhile, provide sufficient flexibility for the user interface to be completely redesigned according to user requirements, although this usually requires more technical expertise and in-depth knowledge of the system. Configuring a system, whether it allows for flexible or only limited configuration, depends on design issues and requires certain decisions to be made. For example, if your system only allows links and logo to be changed, you will need to decide what links you want to create and what logo graphic you want to use. As the creator of a digital collection, your job is to configure the system to expose the underlying functionality and to present the digital content of the collection in a user-friendly format.

In this chapter, we will discuss practical issues related to the user interface design for presenting digital collections using either commercial or open-source digital collection systems.

Importance of user interface design

Arms (2000) notes that 'elegant design, appropriate functionality, and responsive systems make a measurable difference to the effectiveness of digital libraries … A digital library is only as good as the interface it provides to its users'. Without a good user interface, a content-rich digital collection supported by cutting-edge technology may not be accepted by its users. If users find it difficult to navigate the collection, frustrating to find what they are seeking and complicated to view the results, they are unlikely to visit the collection again. Technology alone may not win user acceptance.

The importance of good user interface design can be the difference between user acceptance and rejection of the digital collection. If end users feel it is not easy to learn, not easy to use, or too cumbersome, an otherwise excellent digital collection could fail.

Good user interface design can make a digital collection easy to understand and use, which results in greater user acceptance and interest. This, at some degree, may diminish some imperfect functionality of the digital collection.

The goal of user interface design for digital collections is to develop a web interface to present the functionality and the content of a digital collection to users and to elevate the technical complexity to a user-friendly product. A good user interface design is to make the user's interaction as intuitive as possible. The more intuitive the user interface, the easier it is to use, thus reducing the gulf between users and the application.

Effective user interfaces are visually apparent and forgiving, helping users quickly see the breadth of their options, grasp how to achieve their goals, and do their work. Users should not be concerned with the inner workings of the system (Tognazzini, 2007).

Related issues of user interface design

To design a user interface for a digital collection that is appropriate to the local technical environment and requirements and that satisfies users' needs, the designer should understand several issues.

User needs

User needs are the focus of the design. A design can be successful only when it is based on a deep understanding of the mindset of users. Before starting a user interface design, a designer should ask a series of questions such as, 'Who will be using the digital collection?'; 'How will they use the collection?'; and 'What functions do users want?' Consulting the owning library or selectors of the collection is a good way to understand users' needs as the collection was selected for digitisation for a reason. It may be in high demand so that digitising the collection will provide broader access to the materials. The selectors or the staff members in the owning library have the best knowledge of their users. They understand how the users have used the physical collection and how they would like to use the digital collection. The input from the owning library staff or the selectors is very important for understanding user needs.

The collection

Understanding the content of the collection and the characteristics of the material in the collection will help generate good design ideas that are appropriate for the presentation of the collection. A design for a historical photograph collection will be different from a design for a collection containing mostly books. The former may require appealing graphics or sample photographs showing the content of the collection and simple browsing options and displays. The latter may require hierarchical displays of book titles, chapter titles, and relationships between books and chapters in each book.

Metadata

It would be impossible to design a user interface for a digital collection without understanding the metadata used in the collection. Setting up browse and search options, creating indexes, designing display labels, linking between objects, showing images, and so on, all are built on the metadata. In order to display relevant information, it is important to know which metadata fields are used and which are not used in the collection. Some administrative metadata may not be useful for public users but may be crucial for staff use. For example, archival materials are usually kept in archival boxes and folders. The box number and folder number do not mean anything to the general users. However, searching by box number and folder number is a straightforward way for the staff to locate the physical material. The designer of the user interface must take this into consideration and come up with a solution that meets staff demands but does not annoy general users.

The digital collection system

Understanding the capabilities and limitations of the system on which the digital collection is being built will avoid unrealistic demands and design ideas. For example, if the system does not support hierarchical display of book titles and chapter titles, you will need to design the user interface in an alternative way to accomplish the task using the functions and features that the system does support, rather than spending time experimenting with unrealistic display options.

The structure of the parent website

Usually, a digital collection is not built on an independent website, but may be linked from a library's website, a collaborative digital collections website, or may be a sub-site of a large website. When designing a user interface, the structure and characteristics of the parent website should be studied. The layout, colour scheme, typography of the digital collection should not be strikingly different from the parent site.

Future maintenance issues

Maintaining a digital collection is an important issue. Making changes in and adding new material and metadata records to the current collection may be a routine task. The user interface should not be affected by the changes. When a collection is completed and becomes relatively stable, it will still need to be maintained when the system or the platform is upgraded. Newer versions of the digital collection system or server may affect the configuration of the user interface in the older version. When the parent website is redesigned or upgraded, the digital collection website may need to be changed to fit the structure of the newly designed parent website. When designing a user interface using today's technology and according to today's user needs, it is impossible to predict all future changes and demands. However, it is possible to take this issue into consideration and use appropriate techniques and tools to make future changes more straightforward. For example, using stylesheets to control layout, typography and colours and applying 'server-include' technology for headers and footers reduces the need to make changes in individual collections. Documenting the ideas, methods and technical details in the user interface design will also reduce redundant efforts and save time in future upgrading and maintenance.

Principles of user interface design

Jakob Nielsen, the world's leading expert on user-friendly design, has written a number of books discussing principles of user interface design. His 'Ten usability heuristics' addresses general principles for user interface design (Nielsen, 2005). Bruce Tognazzini's 'First principles of interaction design' also serves as a useful checklist for the principles (Tognazzini, 2007).

Designing a user interface for a digital collection is different from designing a website as it is limited by the technology utilised by the digital collection system or software. For example, if the digital collection software does not support viewing images by thumbnails, it would be redundant to design a user interface with an option of viewing thumbnail images. Nonetheless, some principles of website design are applicable to the user interface design for digital collections.

Simplicity

The design should facilitate simple and common tasks and present features in a clear and simple way. It is important not to complicate the user's task and let the user see clearly what functions are available. The design should communicate clearly and simply in the user's own language.

Visibility

The design should keep all needed options and materials for a given task visible without distracting the user with extraneous or redundant information. Deliver only relevant information and do not overwhelm users with too many alternatives or confuse them with unnecessary information. Make the navigation visible, simple and clear. Avoid invisible navigation.

Consistency

The most important thing in designing a user interface is to ensure it is consistent. The graphic header and footer should be consistent across the collection. The navigation buttons should be in consistent places on all pages. Use the same wording in labels and messages and use a consistent colour scheme throughout the collection. Display metadata records and images in a consistent way so the user can anticipate what will happen when a link is clicked. Apply consistent layout and navigation. Consistency in the user interface enables users to build an accurate mental model of the way it works, so they will not require training and support.

Readability

The onscreen text is a primary source of information for the users. If the text is poorly worded, then the interface will be perceived poorly by the users. Using full words and sentences, as opposed to abbreviations and codes, makes the text easier to understand.

Text that must be read should have high contrast, no matter whether it is on an image or plain text. Use font sizes that are large enough to be readable on standard monitors. Use a different font style for labels and metadata element names to separate them from the metadata text. Use language that users can understand for labels. Use the 'alt' tag for all images and graphic icons so that people who have vision disabilities can read the collection through a reader.

Browsability

Providing browse options is a very important feature for digital collections. Most digital collections are rare or unique, so most people will be unfamiliar with their content. Browsing options will encourage the users to explore and get ideas of how to perform a search. Browsing by categories and by thumbnail images will help users quickly find what they are looking for.

Attractiveness and beauty

While it is not necessary for each digital collection be a work of art, it is important that it is not ugly. The opening page should be attractive and elegant to get users' attention. Appropriate graphics representing the material and content of the collection should be appealing. If possible, apply new technologies that make the presentation and viewing more interesting.

Process of user interface design and configuration

The process of designing a user interface for a digital collection is rather complicated. In some cases, the design process may need to start before digitising the material and creating metadata. This is because some design options may rely on the metadata, especially structural metadata and filenames. There are several steps to complete and implement the user interface design.

Design browse options

Browse options enable users to view digital objects by titles, subjects, personal names, places, categories, types of material, thumbnail images, and other options that can be pulled from the metadata. The browse feature is extremely helpful for users who do not know anything about the collection and do not know how to perform a search.

Determining what to browse and in what sequence to browse will be the focus of the design. Browse options are created from the metadata. Many metadata elements are used to describe each object. However, we do not want to create browse options from all metadata elements included in each record because we do not want to complicate the browse options by presenting irrelevant information. Browse options should be selected from metadata elements based on the following factors:

- *Relevancy*: Select the metadata elements that are relevant for browsing the collection. For example, for most digital collections, relevant browse options may include title, creator, subject, personal name, place, date, and so on, while in most cases, identifier, filename, file location, and so forth, may not be relevant. Of course, in collections where most objects do not have a creator, and thus the metadata element for creator is mostly empty, browsing by creator will be irrelevant. In another collection, filenames may be the best identifiers for retrieving digital objects; here the filename element would become a very important option for browsing.

- *Meaningfulness*: Browse options must be meaningful. For example, if a collection is about Washington, DC, browsing by place name would be meaningless as the place name would be the same. The same holds true for a collection about an illustrator who is the sole creator of the objects in the collection. Here, browsing by creator name would be pointless.

- *User needs*: Sometimes, the owning library requests certain browsing options based on users' special needs. This may require the design of special metadata elements. For example, the Archive of Terror collection (*http://www.aladin.wrlc.org/dl/collection/hdr?terror*) contains about 60,000 metadata records, of which only about 250 have full-text PDF documents attached. A special browse option that lists all PDF documents was designed to meet the needs of the users who want to see full-text documents.

Design search options

Search function enables users to search digital objects in the collection through simple search or advanced search. The design process includes deciding what search engine to use (if the system provides multiple options), what search mode (simple or advanced) to present on the main page, on every page, and on the search page, and what search criteria should be provided on the advanced search mode, and so on. If both simple and advanced searches must be made available to the users, the designer needs to decide how to navigate between the two searching modes.

Design indexes

Indexes make it easier to find specific records and to sort records by the index field. Indexes enable search engines to retrieve the desired records quickly. In digital collections, indexes are created from metadata elements. The index design process must determine what fields to index and what indexes to include in the 'keywords'.

Any metadata field can be indexed. However, indexing all metadata fields may slow down the collection-building. It may also slow down the searching process as the search engine must search more irrelevant information. Selecting appropriate metadata fields for indexing is therefore very important. For example, in a single collection, title, creator, subject, personal name and place name may be good choices for indexing, while collection name, rights, scanning device, scanning location, and so on, may not be good choices for indexing as the information in these fields is the same for all records.

Keyword searching provides the capability of searching across indexes. Keyword searching is essential to users who are not library professionals. Some digital collection systems automatically combine selected indexes and provide keyword searching in the indexed fields. Some systems may require manually selecting indexes to form keywords. When selecting metadata elements for keyword searching, one must be careful to choose meaningful descriptive metadata elements and not include irrelevant information.

In addition to the keyword index, indexes of separate fields are also important for providing advanced search options. In very large collections or combined collections, advanced field search and Boolean search options will provide more accurate and shorter results and speed up the search process. The criteria for metadata elements for indexing for a cross-collection field search are different from those for a single collection search. Some metadata elements, such as collection name and repository name, may not be relevant for indexing a single collection but become relevant in a cross-collection setting. This is because the collection and repository are given in a single collection search, so there is no need to use these elements to restrain the search. A keyword search across all collections, however, will return a great number of hits. In this case, an advanced field search or Boolean search that limits the search to selected fields, such as the collection name or repository, will return better results. In some digital collection systems, such as Greenstone Digital Library Software, the dilemma is that in order to provide a field search for a cross-collection search, the index needs to be set up in the individual collection and may not be relevant in the collection. The solution, in the individual collection, is thus to select meaningful metadata elements for keyword search and set up the keyword search as the default. The indexes for assisting cross-collection search can then be hidden or placed in a less prominent place.

Full-text searching provides the capability to search within the document. In some digital collection systems, such as Greenstone, full-text searching and metadata searching are separate, while other systems may provide a 'keyword anywhere' search that combines full-text and metadata searching.

Design navigation

Navigation assists users to go from one point in a digital collection to another. Navigation design is key to the design process. If it is difficult to go from one point to another, then users will quickly become frustrated and give up. When the flow between screens matches the flow of the work the user is trying to accomplish, then the collection will make sense to the user. Because different users work in different ways, the system needs to be flexible enough to support their various approaches.

A digital collection may include several navigation paths:

- *Navigation within the collection.* This is usually available through browse options, search function and record display. A typical browse option will link the selected item on a browse list to a metadata record that contains a link or a thumbnail image to the large image or document. A typical search result list performs the same path linking an item on the search results to a metadata record. When designing navigation within the collection, the following factors should be considered:

  - *Reduce clicks.* Try to create a way that uses fewer clicks to reach the final destination, i.e. viewing the object.

  - *Provide alternative paths to get the same point.* Browsing options actually provide different ways to get to the same object. Providing links to the same subject, same creator or same series in a record is another alternative path to navigate to the same point. However, too many links within a record may confuse users and dissuade them from continuing.

  - *Provide clear directions and links for the user to go back to where they came from.* Never disable the 'back' button on the browser. According to Nielsen and Loranger (2006), the 'back' button is usually the second most used feature of web browsing.

- *Navigation between collections.* Navigation between collections depends on how the collections are organised and presented. Some digital libraries present all collections in a single user interface and distinguish the collections only by the collection names. In this case, the collection name should be a link to all objects in the collection. Some digital collection websites present each collection individually with slightly different user interfaces and link them together through combined searches. In this case, the search result list should indicate the collection name and the owning library. In general, a user may not care about what collection an object belongs to and where it came from. However, a serious researcher will need to have such information in order to correctly cite the website and/or the digital object or contact the owning library for more information. In addition, a 'transfer point' i.e. a collaborative webpage listing all collections should be created and each individual collection should have a link to the 'transfer point' and to navigate to another collection.

- *Navigation to the parent website.* It is necessary to provide navigation to the parent website and the organisation(s) of the collection owner. This is usually accomplished by using consistent headers and footers, side bars, icons, and so on.

Design displays

Display design includes the following elements:

- *Display of browse lists.* How should a browse option be presented to the user? Should thumbnail images be used for a title browse list? Should different icons be used for different types of materials? Should a title browse list include brief metadata? How should a hierarchical list be presented to the user? How should dates be displayed, e.g. numerically, such as 1898-02-18 or spelled out in full, such as February 18, 1898? These are just few of the issues to be decided when designing displays for browse lists. The browse displays must be clear and meaningful and provide right and relevant information to the users. Uncommonly used abbreviations and acronyms must be spelled out. This may require using a script to convert the abbreviations and acronyms in the metadata to the full names in the display.

- *Display of search results.* How should search results be presented to users? How should they be sorted? Alphabetically by title, by relevance, or by both according to the user's choice? Should thumbnails with brief metadata be included in the search results? Should different icons be used for different documents on the search results screen? How many hits should be displayed on the screen? Should the search term be highlighted on the search results? These are some of the questions to be answered when designing a display for a search result list. According to Nielsen (2008), 'users are incredibly bad at interpreting SERP listings (SERP = Search Engine Results Page)'. To help users understand the search results in a digital collection, the search results page must be designed to present information in a user-friendly manner.

- *Display of a record.* Record display may include detailed information about a digital object. Should the record be displayed in a brief version, a detailed version, or according to the user's preference? What information should be displayed in the record? Should the record include a link to the full document or display the document or image and the record side by side? Should the record include a thumbnail image linking to the large image or multiple images? These are some of the issues to be decided when designing a record display. Displaying metadata records is an advantage of digital collections created by libraries, and helps researchers locate information about particular digital objects, contact the owning library for more information, and correctly cite the item in their research.

- *Display of digital objects.* Displaying digital objects is a very important feature of a digital collection – after all, this is what the users want to see. How should images or other types of digital object be displayed? What dimensions should be used? Should full-version images be displayed in a new window? How should multiple-page documents, such as manuscripts, letters and newspaper clippings be displayed? The presentation software used for the digital collection plays a key role in deciding how to display the digital objects. For example, if the software does not support zooming, you will need to design an alternative display for viewing the details of a large-format image.

- *Display labels.* Labels are used for displaying metadata elements, links and images. Although some metadata sets provide display labels for elements, they are unlikely to meet the specific needs of a collection. For example, 'coverage' is the official label for the Dublin Core element of the same name. If we use the qualified Dublin Core element 'coverage.spatial', we may need to change the label to 'place name' which is more specific and less confusing for users.

Design preferences

Most digital collection presentation systems provide preferences to allow users to select their preferred mode or format for searching and browsing. Search preferences may include query mode (i.e. simple vs. advanced), query style, (i.e. normal with a single search box vs. fielded with several fields in a form), case differences (i.e. ignore case differences vs. upper/lower case must match), word endings (i.e. ignore word endings vs. whole word must match), accent differences (i.e. ignore accents vs. accents must match), search history (i.e. display search history vs. do not display search history), and maximum number of hits returned and number of hits per page. Browsing preferences may include language choice, browse by a list or by thumbnail images, and so on.

Selecting and setting up appropriate default options is very important as most users do not bother selecting preferences unless the default setting is not good. The default setting may be different in a small single digital collection compared with in a large or cross-collection search. For example, the default search option 'ignore case differences' in a small single collection may work perfectly, but in a large or cross-collection search, this may result in too many hits. Users may need to select 'upper/lower case must match' option to get the desired results.

Design graphics

Good graphic design is eye catching and attractive. Graphic design may be utilised to apply a theme or style to the interface without compromising its intuitive usability.

Nielsen and Tahir (2002) recommend showcasing sample content on the homepage. This can be represented by selected images from the digital collection. Users should be able to see and to understand what kinds of materials and content are included in the digital collection through well designed homepage graphics and graphic headers.

Before starting graphic design for a digital collection, get ideas by looking at similar websites. Examine closely what others have done and what grabs or eludes your attention and why. In addition, look at all images in the collection to select eye-catching ones to represent the collection. The staff at the owning library or the selectors of the collection are a good source for recommending good graphics because they are familiar with the content in their collections.

When appropriate, the graphic design for a digital collection should incorporate the logo of the owing library and the colour scheme of the owning library's website. Graphic design should be consistent across all digital collections and must be visually appealing.

Typography and layout

Typography is an art concerned with design elements that can be applied to the letters and text. As Nielsen and Loranger (2006) point out, typography and colour schemes play an important part in making a good first impression with your website. Typography gives users a feeling for your organisation and conveys an idea of what they might achieve via the site. Designing good typography for a digital collection's website will give users a good first impression. The rules and recommendations regarding typography for a website are also applicable for a digital collection website.

Typography is mainly concerned with the style and size of typefaces. A complete set of type of the same style and size is called a font. 'Different fonts can signify whimsy or gravity, and point size and colour can emphasise content. Sustaining positive impression throughout the site means choosing the type and colours that work best on the web' (Nielsen and Loranger, 2006). Generally speaking, readers prefer to read in 12-point type. As a rule, anything larger than 14-point seems loud and aggressive, while anything smaller than 10-point looks tiny and forbidding. Nielsen and Loranger therefore recommend keeping body text no smaller than 10-point. In addition, avoid anti-aliasing for text smaller than 12-point (Nielsen and Loranger, 2006). Use style attributes (e.g. bold, italic, underlining, etc.) appropriately. Too many font enhancements and typographic twists on a single page can actually distract or anaesthetise the reader's attention and dilute emphasis.

Text and background contrast is another issue for design. Low contrast can cause eye strain and discomfort. Black text on a white background will make it easier to read.

A layout is a design for the overall appearance of a website with particular emphasis on the effective positioning and arrangement of page elements. The most important consideration in page layout is spacing. Crowded and busy screens are difficult to understand and, hence, difficult to use. Webpages that are covered top-to-bottom, side-to-side, and corner-to-corner with thick, crowded, undifferentiated text are hard to use.

Typography and layout design demands the design and creation of a stylesheet. Using a stylesheet for the web interface makes it easy to maintain and to make changes in the future. A generic stylesheet can be used for all digital collections to keep consistency.

Create a mock-up

After all design decisions are made, it is very helpful to create a mock-up to illustrate the design ideas. A mock-up is a working sample for reviewing. Mock-ups are used by designers mainly to acquire feedback from users about design ideas early in the design process.

Creating a screen mock-up or mock-ups for the user interface of a digital collection can convey the flavour of the design. Although the mock-ups may not be functional, they are essential for comparing alternatives and resolving certain issues. Realistic colour mock-ups help the designer and reviewers visualise different design alternatives. Through mock-ups, a designer can test different colour schemes and different layouts and make the final decision on the design.

Using Adobe Photoshop to create mock-ups is easy as it can store a layered image in PSD format. The layered PSD file separates each design element in different layers and allows each individual element to be edited separately. This is extremely important when incorporating several images into one graphic and creating text on the graphic. If one part of the final graphic needs to be changed or the text needs to be changed, the change can be made on the individual graphic layer or the text layer without recreating the whole graphic. The layers can be displayed and hidden, which provides an easy visual tool to switch between alternative images to optimise the final design.

Configure the system

System configuration implements the user interface design and enables all the designed functionality. Almost all digital collection systems provide custom configuration at a certain level. Some systems are easy to configure but may not be flexible enough to accommodate all design ideas. Some systems are very flexible but may not be easy to configure. It is very important to understand the capability of the system configuration before designing a user interface for a digital collection.

System configuration should start when a small number of documents and metadata records are available. Using the small pool of documents and metadata records as a testing bed makes it easy to adjust the design and experiment with the configuration. If the system configuration cannot be completed until the documents and metadata records are created, then, if the system allows, it is wise to first upload a small number of documents and metadata records to test the configuration settings.

Test and evaluate the user interface

After the test site's system configuration is completed, a complete test should be conducted to evaluate each function and requirement that has been designed. Check display labels and text for accuracy. Make sure metadata is adequate and accurate, pay attention to those metadata elements required for every record, such as ownership statement, copyright information, and so on. These elements are usually put in a template that is used to create all records. Some digital collection systems may not have the capability to make global changes. Once records are created, the field data cannot be changed all at once. Catching errors in the early stages of production will save time and money compared with correcting the errors at a late stage. The test process will ensure this issue.

Navigation should also be tested thoroughly. Make sure all links on the header and footer are working and the image links are correct. Links within a record or on a browse list go where they supposed to go.

Search testing is also important. Try searching in different ways and in different modes (simple and advanced) and make sure the results are accurate, the ranking is correct and the display of searching results is correct as designed.

Invite staff and users to test and evaluate the test collection and get feedback. Make changes as requested before rolling out the final product.

Documenting the process

The design process is completed with detailed documentation. The documentation should list the design ideas for functionality, display, layout, the problems experienced, and the solution conducted. The documentation should also record the design ideas that were not implemented for whatever reason, as this will help reduce redundant efforts in the design process for future collections.

Case study: designing the user interface for the DCPC's digital collections

The WRLC member libraries maintain a variety of unique special collections that have been and will be digitised in DCPC or hosted in the DCPC's digital collections, which are presented through the WRLC Digital Collections interface (*http://www.aladin.wrlc.org/dl*). The types of material include manuscripts, photographs, slides, full-text documents, newspaper clippings, magazines, comic books, audio recordings, scrapbooks and others. Due to the consortium libraries' participation in various overlapping projects and systems, each digital collection must be independent. It is very important to make the libraries' digital collections available across multiple environments and accessible through multiple channels. The libraries may use individual digital objects outside the WRLC digital library system for online exhibits or other purposes. Each digital object and its related metadata must be independently accessible and in standard formats in order to be linked from other online systems (Zhang and Gourley, 2003). To provide good support for users to use the digital collections, we put considerable effort into customising and enhancing the generic user interface.

The standard Greenstone user interface

The Greenstone Library Software we use provides browse options and supports indexing and full-text searching. Each collection can be built independently using Greenstone so that individual collections can be linked from other online systems and used for other purposes.

Greenstone's user interface is workable and configurable, but in its default form it is rather basic. We focused on customising the Greenstone interface to highlight the unique features of the individual digital collections.

The standard Greenstone user interface displays a header, either graphic or plain text, with navigation buttons to help, preferences and home. Below the header is a navigation bar that contains search and browse options. Under the navigation bar is a main display area that can be used to display the browse lists, search results, and metadata record or full-text document. We have adopted most elements of the standard Greenstone user interface for all our collections, but have created different browsing options, indexes, display labels and graphics for different collections.

In all of the DCPC collections, the metadata description is presented in a standard library OPAC format with a thumbnail image linking to the actual document. Full-sized images can be viewed with Image Viewer in another browser window. Scrapbooks can be viewed through a Flash plug-in. Full-text transcriptions in any format are linked within the record and can be viewed through appropriate applications such as MS Word and PDF reader.

We designed a header that is consistent across all collections, and contains a help button, a button to return to the main page of the collection, and a link to the WRLC Digital Collections webpage.

The footer format is also consistent across all collections, with text links to the main page of the collection, help, preferences, a link to the WRLC Digital Collections, and a link to the owning library's website.

Designing and customising browse options

Greenstone allows the setting up of browse options by creating a 'classifier' using any metadata element. We set up browse options according to the content and metadata of the collection. For most collections, the browse options are created for titles, subjects, creators, places, people, dates, and so on. Some collections do not contain all the metadata. For example, the metadata in the Drew Pearson's 'Washington Merry-Go-Round' Collection (*http://www.aladin.wrlc.org/dl/collection/ hdr?pearson*) was generated automatically by the filenames, and only two metadata elements (title and date) are available for browsing. Some collections request more browsing options for particular content. For example, The John R. Hickman Collection (*http://www.aladin.wrlc .org/dl/collection/hdr?hickman*) consists of broadcast-quality audio recordings of vintage radio news and entertainment programmes from the 1920s through the 1970s. In addition to browse options by titles, subjects, people and dates, it requires a browse option by 'programmes'. This option is set up to display the radio programmes in a hierarchical list sorted by the main programmes and subcategories under each programme.

The display labels for the browsing options are also different based on the content and metadata in each collection. For example, the display label 'organizations' represents the metadata element 'DC.Subject.corpname' for topical corporate names. In the Federal Theatre Project Poster, Costume, and Set Design Slide Collection (*http://www.aladin.wrlc.org/ dl/collection/hdr?ftpp*), the 'DC.Subject.corpname' field contains theatre names, so these were labelled 'theaters', as this was more clear and specific than the label 'organizations'.

Designing and setting up indexes

Index setup is flexible in the Greenstone system. Indexes can be created from any metadata elements. We created a keyword index to combine all relevant metadata elements for keyword searching, which is consistent in all DCPC digital collections. In each collection, we created different indexes according to the content and user needs. For example, as the staff members in special collections and archives feel it is convenient and much easier to search documents by their locations, so we created an index based on the location metadata to search by 'box and folder' numbers. This option is placed at the lower level of the search options so it will not affect searches conducted by general public users. In the Greenstone system, metadata index and full-text index are separated, which may be considered as one of the drawbacks of the system. To overcome this, in the digital collections that contain all full-text documents, we put the full-text search option at the top of the search option list as the default for users to search 'anywhere' in the collection. We also created some hidden indexes to facilitate linking between digital objects within a single collection.

Designing and customising navigation

Besides the standard Greenstone navigation, we designed specific navigations for the collections that require additional features. For example, for the *Treasure Chest of Fun and Fact* (*http://www.aladin .wrlc.org/dl/collection/hdr?treasure*) Collection, we designed structural metadata to facilitate the navigation. In the Greenstone system, we used conditional format statements in the configuration file to display the metadata according to the record type, i.e. whether it is a story record or an issue record. When a story title is clicked from the title list, a story record is displayed with the first thumbnail image in the story. When the thumbnail in the record is clicked, all images attached to this single story can be viewed through the Image Viewer program. Figure 7.1 illustrates the story record and navigation.

When an 'issue' link is clicked, the issue record is displayed with a link to the table of contents and a cover image of the issue. The user can click the table of contents to view each story or click the cover image to view

Figure 7.1 Story record display and navigation

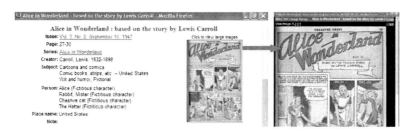

Figure 7.2 Issue record display and navigation

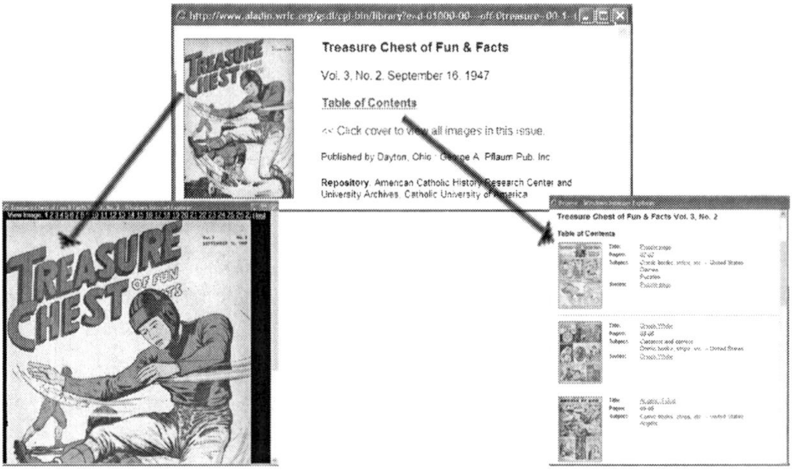

all images in this issue. Figure 7.2 demonstrates the issue record display and navigation.

Designing and modifying displays

By modifying the Greenstone configuration file, we set up different title display lists for different materials. For example, for collections containing photographs and images, the title list displays thumbnails of the photographs or images with brief descriptions; for collections containing manuscripts or documents, the title list displays a small icon with the title; for PDF documents, the title list displays a PDF icon with the title; and for sound recordings, the title list displays a sound icon with the title.

Some of our member libraries decided to digitise some of the historical scrapbooks in their collections. The scrapbooks contain photographs, newspaper clippings, cards, three-dimensional objects, brochures, small booklets, and other objects. Many of the newspaper clippings and other objects are layered on top of each other and the brochures and small booklets contain multiple pages that are not visible when viewed from a normal display screen. To address this issue, we created a Flash application that applies animations to the scrapbook so that the pages can be turned like flipping a real book.

The final online scrapbook provides a user-friendly interface. Users can flip the pages by clicking or dragging the mouse, typing the page number, or clicking the 'next' and 'previous' button on the book's navigation bar. The user can zoom in to see details of each page. Each highlighted item can be clicked so that a larger version of the object is displayed in another window with title description. The small booklets can also be viewed using the page-flipping feature. The online scrapbook displays page numbers as well as the total number of pages in the book. Figure 7.3 shows a screenshot of the final online scrapbook. Arrow 1 shows that when a booklet is clicked, a flippable booklet is opened in another window. Arrow 2 points to a highlighted item as a user selects it using the mouse. Arrows 3 and 4 indicate when a highlighted item has been clicked and a larger version of the image is displayed in another window with title information (Zhang, 2007).

Figure 7.3   Screenshot of the online scrapbook

Designing and creating graphical homepages and headers

As all of our digital collections are independently built, we have the flexibility to design graphics based on the content and subject of each collection. When designing the graphics for each collection, we follow the following rules:

- all collections should have similar-looking but different flavours, representing content, subjects and material types of the specific collection;

- when possible, images should be selected from the collection as a showcase;

- opening page graphics should be eye-catching and attractive;

- all collections should have the same banner at the top, linking to the consortial digital library;

- when possible, the design, typography and the colour scheme should look similar to the owning library's website.

Following are some examples of the graphic design:

- *George Washington University Historical Photographs* (Figure 7.4; *http://www.aladin.wrlc.org/dl/collection/hdr?gwhist*). The collection contains photographs and negatives of individuals, localities, objects, buildings, events and groups associated with the history of the university, representing a photographic timeline of The George Washington University from approximately 1859 through the late 1980s.

- *Federal Theatre Project Poster, Costume, and Set Design Slide Collection* (Figure 7.5; *http://www.aladin.wrlc.org/dl/collection/ hdr?ftpp*). The collection contains nearly 1,000 35-mm slides taken

Figure 7.4 Graphic design for the George Washington University Historical Photographs Collection

Figure 7.5 Graphic design for the Federal Theatre Project Poster, Costume, and Set Design Slide Collection

Figure 7.6 Graphic design for the Charles Munroe Papers Collection

from original posters that were created by the Federal Theatre Project (FTP). These images are of the original designs used on posters to advertise FTP plays in many different US cities from 1935 to 1939.

- *Charles Munroe Papers* (Figure 7.6; *http://www.aladin.wrlc.org/dl/ collection/hdr?munroe*). Charles Munroe (1849–1938), the inventor of smokeless gunpowder, was head of the Department of Chemistry and the Dean of the Corcoran Scientific School at Columbian University (which became George Washington University in 1904) between 1892 and 1898. This collection contains the correspondence, articles, lecture notes, newspaper clippings, notebooks and photographs of Charles Munroe, from 1882 to 1936.

8

The complete digitisation process and workflow management

Creating digital collections is a complex process consisting of several major stages. Each stage has its particular workflow. In previous chapters, we discussed issues in each stage of the digitisation process. In this chapter, we will summarise the digitisation process and discuss workflow management.

A typical digitisation process is as illustrated in Figure 8.1.

Project planning is the first stage to start a digitisation project. The planning process varies from project to project. Large collaborative projects may involve several institutions, require large funding, and can take years to plan. Small projects conducted by a single institution may involve a few people and the planning process can be very simple and quick. Regardless of the project's size, any digitisation project must go through a planning process.

Selecting the physical material for digitising is an essential stage in the digitisation process. Without selecting this material, the project does not exist. Some digitisation projects categorise the selection process in the planning stage. No matter whether the selecting process is included in the planning process or stands on its own, it is an indispensable step in the digitisation process.

Establishing an efficient metadata strategy can ensure proper descriptions of the digital objects, achieve desired file structure for components of the digital objects, speed up metadata creation, and benefit interoperability and future maintenance. Although selecting a metadata standard for a digitisation project is a very important issue, designing metadata is overlooked in many digitisation projects. Selecting the metadata schema that best suits the project and organisational needs is undoubtedly key for metadata creation. However, designing structural metadata and a file naming convention and developing a digital object content model are also very important.

Figure 8.1 Digitisation process

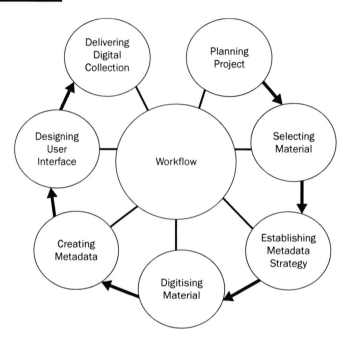

Digitising material is at the core of the digitisation project – after all, the whole point of a digitisation project is the conversion of material from physical format to digital format. As such, it may be mistakenly considered as the most complex and most expensive process in a digitisation project. The term 'scanning project' has been used interchangeably for 'digitisation project', implying that scanning is the only process in digitisation. In fact, planning the project, selecting material and establishing the metadata strategy are more complicated than scanning. Through thoughtful project planning, careful material selection and preparation, and effective metadata strategy, the scanning process may be very easy and straightforward, no matter whether it is done in-house or by an external vendor. In most cases, scanning alone is not always the most expensive process – metadata creation may cost more than scanning.

Metadata creation is another focus of digitisation projects, although many people beginning a digitisation project do overlook this. Manual metadata creation can be very expensive and time-consuming. When possible, computer-assisted metadata creation should be considered and designed.

User interface design may also be neglected, as some digital collection systems provide a default end-user interface. In a large ongoing collaborative project, the structure and user interface may be stable, and each new collection submitted by participating institutions may be added to the project for display through the same user interface. Organisations participating in such collaborative projects may well consider the user interface design not to be part of their digitisation project. However, in order to brand the digital collection with organisational characteristics and demands, the default user interface must be configured to meet the organisational needs. A digital collection cannot be delivered to end users without a customised user interface.

Delivering the digital collection to the end user is the last step of the process. Although most digital collections created by libraries are delivered through the web and open to the general public, some collections may be restricted to a group of users and/or a specified place (e.g. on campus) and therefore require alternative delivery methods, such as CD-ROM, DVD, dedicated workstations, and the like.

Workflow management

The complete digitisation process describes what needs to be done but does not demonstrate how each stage is to be completed, who will do it, and in what sequence. Workflow management answers these questions. Workflow is a process and/or procedure in which tasks are completed.

All digitisation projects will go through the digitisation process, but each project may have a different workflow. As discussed in Chapter 2, workflow management is a very important part of project planning. Knowing what to do in what order and making sure that the inputs for each step are available when that step is performed will benefit efficient workflow. Most grant-funded projects require more thoughtful workflow management because the projects likely have strict timelines and usually hire temporary project staff. Most projects that have not been completed on time have suffered from inefficient workflow management. In most cases, the projects have to find extra funding and allocate staff time to finish the projects. According to the Library of Congress Ameritech National Digital Library Competition (1996–1999), the need to adjust workflow was one of the important lessons learned by the project awardees (Library of Congress, 1999).

Workflow management varies from project to project and from institution to institution. Bauer and Walls observed workflow at Cornell University Library and Harvard University Library and summarise as follows:

> A key divergence between Cornell and Harvard seems to be that Harvard employs a more decentralized workflow than Cornell. Separate units do work, although much of it eventually moves through the impressive digitization space in Widener Library. The difference has seemed to be that Harvard has a very large pot of money that is allowing them to do more digitization in more places. Cornell has had to create a more efficient and centralized system because they need to recoup costs through charging back. (Bauer and Walls, 2005)

As illustrated in Figure 8.1, workflow connects all major stages of a digitisation process together. There are different levels of workflow management. The highest level of workflow management is to make arrangements for the major stages of the digitisation project. It is especially important to those collaborative projects which involve people from different departments and different institutions working on different tasks. The workflow must be made clear to all people involved – they should be informed of what they need to do, in what sequence, when they should finish their tasks, and what the expected outcome should be. A good way to achieve this is with a table of schedules and timelines with the names of those assigned responsibilities. The second level of workflow management is to determine workflow for each task, such as workflow for scanning and image processing, workflow for metadata creation, and so on. More detailed step-by-step instructions may be considered as the lower-level workflow management that is essential to accomplish each task. Documenting the detailed workflow will benefit the management of the project, especially when projects are simultaneous.

Before starting a digitisation project, draft a list of major tasks that need to be completed, and then determine who will do what and in what order. As all institutions have different organisational structures, budgets, IT support, and hardware and software, and staff have different expertise and skills, workflow management for digitisation projects will differ from place to place. Even similar projects have different workflows in different institutions – there is no standard workflow model.

Below is a sample list of tasks we need to accomplish for a simple photograph collection from one institution.

Planning

- Communicate with the owning library to identify
  - purpose and goals of the project;
  - the scope of the project, i.e. whether it is a complete collection or a part of the collection;
  - size of the collection, i.e. number of photographs;
  - if there are any oversized photographs;
  - needs for special care for the photographs;
  - if there are any copyright issues;
  - if there are any use restrictions;
  - format of accompanying metadata, if any;
  - project deadline;
  - contact person.
- Communicate with internal IT department to arrange for storage space, if needed.
- Develop a project plan including target timelines for delivering material and accompanying metadata and relevant information.
- Send the project plan to the owning library for approval.
- Send a copyright clearance form for the owning library to sign.
- Arrange for material delivery.
- Plan workflow.

Selecting material

- Develop selection criteria.
- Select material.
- Research copyright issue if needed.
- Prepare the material – labelling, packaging, metadata, etc.
- Deliver material to the scanning facility.

Establishing metadata strategy

- Review original material and all relevant information.
- Outline options for browse and search.

- Decide what to include in the descriptive and administrative metadata.
- Design file naming convention.
- Design structural metadata – relations.
- Decide if it is possible to create metadata records automatically.
- Document the design ideas.

Digitising material

- Determine scanning techniques.
- Scan images and save as master files according to designed file naming convention.
- Perform quality control.
- Batch processing images to
    - embed metadata in the master file;
    - add ownership information to each image;
    - convert master files to display files and thumbnails.
- Rename files if needed.
- Record scanning statistics.

Creating metadata

- Create metadata and assign subject headings.
- Check metadata records to assure quality.
- Develop crosswalk between metadata formats if needed.
- Develop instructions to create metadata automatically, if desired.
- Submit metadata and digital images to the digital object catalogue.
- Record statistics for metadata creation.

Designing and configuring the user interface

- Review descriptions of the collection.
- Review digital images in the collection and select images for collection homepage and graphic header.
- Review metadata.

- Identify user needs and organisational needs.
- Identify display requirements.
- Design browse and index options.
- Design graphics and create a mock-up.
- Configure the system.
- Import metadata and digital images to Greenstone Digital Library Software.
- Build the collection using Greenstone.

Delivering digital collection

- Add the collection to the WRLC digital collections website.
- Notify the owning library.
- Summarise the project.
- Send a report to the owning library.
- Create a collection-level MARC record in the consortial catalogue.
- Announce the collection in appropriate media.
- Return material to owning library.

Efficient workflow utilises manpower, equipment and time smartly. Efficient workflow goes through each task and step logically and smoothly without any interruption or time wasting. An efficient workflow does not require finishing one task and starting another task after. Some tasks may require steps to be taken in an exact order while some do not. Therefore, some tasks may start in the middle of the previous task and some tasks can progress simultaneously. For example, as soon as the file naming convention is determined, the scanning can start while continuing structural metadata design. Scanning, file conversion, and image processing can be done in groups, i.e. scan and process a small amount of images at a time so that the metadata creation can start. Once some metadata records are created, the interface design process can start.

A detailed workflow for each task also needs to be managed. As each digital collection contains different types of material and has different metadata, each major task of the digitisation process may require a different workflow. The following examples illustrate the workflow for the same task – metadata creation for two digitisation projects.

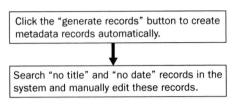

Figure 8.2 Workflow of metadata creation for the Pearson Collection

> Click the "generate records" button to create metadata records automatically.

> Search "no title" and "no date" records in the system and manually edit these records.

Example 1: Drew Pearson's 'Washington Merry-Go-Round'

As described in Chapter 6, this collection contains typescript copies of articles for the 'Washington Merry-Go-Round' newspaper column (*http:// www.aladin.wrlc.org/dl/collection/hdr?pearson*). We created searchable PDF documents from the typescripts. The articles have consistent titles that can be divided into several categories. We designed a file naming convention to include date, article category and page sequence. The metadata records were created automatically using a script based on the filename. For instances when an article's title or date could not be identified, we assigned a letter in the filename to tell the script to fill in the title with 'no title' or 'no date'. These records then were edited manually. The metadata creation workflow was very simple as most of the work was done automatically by a computer. The workflow is illustrated in Figure 8.2.

Example 2: *Treasure Chest of Fun and Fact*

As described in Chapter 4, the *Treasure Chest of Fun and Fact* is a comic book collection (*http://www.aladin.wrlc.org/dl/collection/hdr?treasure*). We decided to create a metadata record for each article and create a record for each issue. Structural metadata was designed to link the articles to the issue. Browse options included titles, creators, subjects, people and series, to show article record and display images from each article. Another browse option was to browse by issue, which could be used to show issue records in chronological order. Each issue could be viewed from cover to cover and through the table of contents.

The workflow for metadata creation involved three staff members and the steps were followed in precise order so that the digital object management system could automatically and correctly include the

Figure 8.3 Workflow of metadata creation for the Treasure Chest Collection

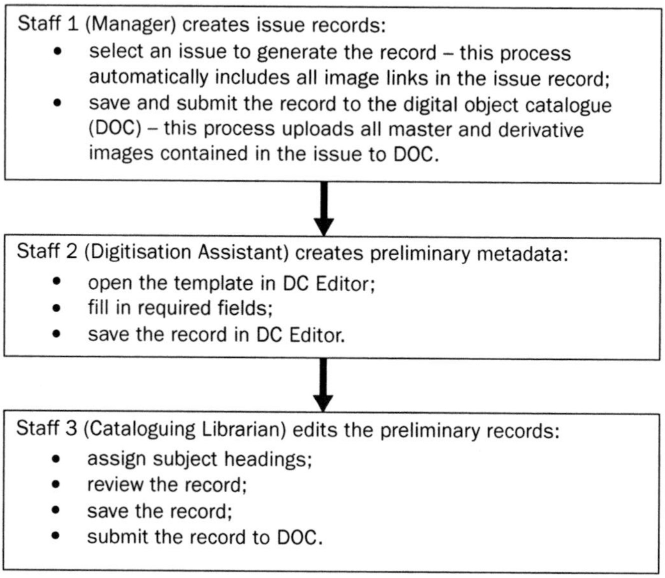

Staff 1 (Manager) creates issue records:
- select an issue to generate the record – this process automatically includes all image links in the issue record;
- save and submit the record to the digital object catalogue (DOC) – this process uploads all master and derivative images contained in the issue to DOC.

Staff 2 (Digitisation Assistant) creates preliminary metadata:
- open the template in DC Editor;
- fill in required fields;
- save the record in DC Editor.

Staff 3 (Cataloguing Librarian) edits the preliminary records:
- assign subject headings;
- review the record;
- save the record;
- submit the record to DOC.

images relevant to each article and establish relations between articles and issues. Figure 8.3 illustrates the workflow.

Some software packages provide tools to manage detailed workflow for some tasks, such as OCR, image processing, metadata creation, user management, file movement and archiving, and so on. When selecting and using this kind of software, you should be aware that it may not be flexible to meet all your organisational needs and specific workflow requirements, as demonstrated in Example 2.

Prototyping and quality control

In Chapter 2, we discussed the importance of prototyping. We want to address this issue again with workflow management. Having learned from our own experience, we strongly recommend the prototyping process for each digitisation project. One lesson we learned was from a large digitisation project that had started several years prior. The scanning was performed by student workers and the owning library had not established any mechanism for quality control. The project kept going for three years without testing or prototyping. When we took over this project, we found that the quality of the images was very poor. We had to rescan 20 per cent of the images and retouch over 80 per cent of the images in the collection. The metadata was also created by student workers without professional instructions. Cleaning up the metadata records went on for several years after the collection was built. Had this project gone through a prototyping process it would have avoided all the rescan and cleaning trouble and saved a lot of time and money.

Testing may be performed at any stage and with any individual task. For example, to determine scanning techniques, it is wise to scan some samples at different resolutions, bit-depths and colours for testing purposes. To decide what structural metadata should be used to connect related images, experimental metadata records can be created for testing.

Figure 8.4 illustrates the prototyping process.

Quality control may be performed during scanning, image processing and metadata creation. It is important to get examples of the desired quality for scanned images and metadata records.

The prototyping process will provide the opportunity to adjust workflow arrangements and to make changes in scanning technique and metadata creation before rolling out full production. Rearranging

Figure 8.4　Prototyping process

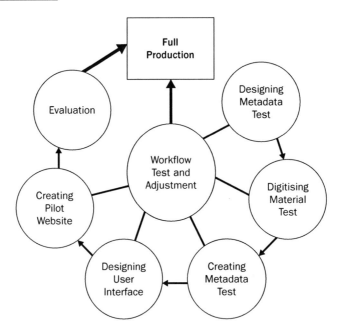

workflow based on the observations and testing results during the prototyping process may be necessary. Adjusting workflow at an early stage may speed up the project.

It is important to understand that no matter how carefully the project is planned, surprises will happen due to changes in technology, staff turnover and unexpected circumstances. Be prepared, flexible and responsive.

Maintenance

As mentioned in Chapter 2, maintenance is one of the key components of digitisation. We did not include maintenance in the digitisation production cycle because it is part of the digitisation lifecycle. It involves issues after the digital collection is created and delivered to the users. Maintenance is always an issue for grant-funded digitisation projects. After the project is completed and the funding has dried up, who should maintain the project will often become an issue.

Maintaining a digital collection is a long-term task. It may involve the following:

- make corrections in metadata records such as typos, incorrect and inconsistent subjects and personal names, etc.;
- fix missing images and incorrect page numbers;
- fix broken links;
- add more images and metadata;
- change information on the homepage;
- migrate to newer software and hardware;
- preserve the digital assets;
- collect and report use statistics.

It is essential to have a maintenance plan and allocate staff and time for maintaining digital collections.

9

Digital collections management system

In previous chapters we described the processes involved in creating and managing digital collections, and discussed major issues in each stage of the digitisation process. In this chapter, we will describe the computer tools and components that support those processes, such as digitisation equipment and software, programs for creating metadata and combining with content files, storage devices, and systems for presenting digital collections on the web. When integrated and coupled together, we refer to these tools and components collectively as a *digital collections management system* (DCMS).

The digital collections production chain

The digitisation and other processes we have described for producing a digital collection form a production chain. This is a kind of 'value chain', a concept from business management that describes a chain of activities through which a product passes, with each activity adding some value to the product (Porter, 1985). A digital collection production chain starts with production services (digitisation, encoding, derivative production, metadata entry) resulting in the creation of digital objects that have more value than their independent constituent parts (content files and metadata records). Storing and organising the objects into a digital collection is the next value-adding activity in the chain. Presenting or publishing the collection on the web through an effective user interface adds even more value to the collection. The end product in this example is an assemblage of several components, including digital images (content files), descriptions about the images (metadata records), a storage system, and a user interface. Figure 9.1 illustrates the major components of this production chain.

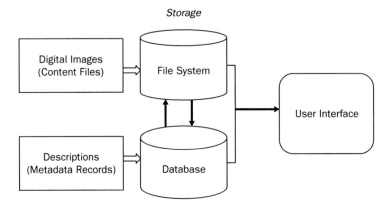

Figure 9.1   Components of a digital collection production chain

In its simplest form, the production chain produces a digital collection that is just a set of computer files and a web server to deliver them to the user. Hyperlinks and image tags connect the metadata and content files. Some of the first digital collections put on the web relied on hand-coded HTML to establish these links. As the number and size of collections grew it became clear that software was needed to manage and organise the files, to create, for example, indexes to support searching. Programs were also used to dynamically create webpages for individual digital objects to support, for example, navigation through multiple content files. Still, early digitisation projects relied heavily on manual inputs and custom programming for these tasks. The functions and features of these collections were limited due to a lack of advanced indexing and user interface technology. Scalability, interoperability and maintenance became ongoing issues for these early digitisation projects.

Today there are software applications that can dramatically simplify the process of digital collection creation, file organisation, indexing and web delivery. These programs can integrate the components of a digital collection seamlessly and efficiently. Some software can automatically manage the digital image and metadata creation workflow. Some programs provide powerful indexing, searching and file management functionality. Other systems provide tools for creating dynamic webpages with efficient discovery and navigation features for finding and viewing the digital collection. More recently, it is being recognised that the value chain for digital collections should not stop at the production of a single user interface but can continue by accessing, repurposing and recombining the content in new and different contexts. To enable this kind of reuse, access services need to be well defined and not embedded in a particular user interface or presentation system. A repository, i.e. a set of services implemented over the storage system, can help achieve this.

The technology supporting the functions required for digital collection production chains make up the DCMS. The DCMS functions include:

- creation (e.g. scanning, OCR, metadata creation);
- management (e.g. adding/deleting/modifying objects, collection description);
- discovery (e.g. indexing, searching, harvesting of content and/or metadata);
- presentation (e.g. collection websites, object dissemination tools);
- preservation (e.g. archiving, migrating).

The hardware and software components of a DCMS include scanners or other digitisation equipment, software tools for entering or generating metadata and linking it with content files to create a digital object, computer storage systems to hold the digital objects, a repository for defining and archiving collections, software to index and search the index, web servers for publishing collections and web browsers for accessing them, and software tools for viewing or playing specialised multimedia content. To ensure the most efficient workflow and processes throughout the lifecycle of a digital collection, the components need to be integrated with each other. However, the integration should be loosely coupled, with components invoked through well-defined interfaces as needed rather than being compiled up front into a monolithic system, so that the DCMS functions, and the value chains they support, can evolve and expand.

Digital collections management system technology

Technology refers to the design, architecture and components that make up the DCMS. The software standards, frameworks and application programming interfaces used to build the system can have an enormous effect on the overall flexibility and scalability of the system. There are several aspects of system technology that should be considered when implementing a DCMS:

- openness;
- scalability;
- reliability;

- flexibility;
- platform.

There are three levels of *openness*, each implying, but not required for, openness of the next levels: source, services and data. Open source, discussed in more detail in Chapter 10, means that the source code used to compile the system can be viewed, modified and distributed freely. This implies that other levels of the architecture, services and data, are also open, although direct access may require system programming.

Open services mean that the system functionality can be invoked directly without going through the user interface. This can be done without open source if an open published application program interface (API) is available. APIs can provide powerful tools for integrating the components of a DCMS, such as workflow applications, the repository and web servers. Another common mechanism for opening up system services is to provide plug-in interfaces. Plug-ins are software components that add new functionality to an application. These components are independently 'pluggable', that is, they can be dropped in, removed or modified without the need to modify other modules. Plug-ins can be used to create an API for system integration if an appropriate one is not part of the DCMS.

Open services are essential for integrating diverse applications into a cohesive DCMS, whether this integration is done by a vendor or in-house. They generally require some programming skill to exploit, although we are seeing simple web APIs in network applications that are quite easy to use. For example, a repository or web portal might provide a syndication interface that can be customised with basic XML transformation techniques. XML-based web APIs make it increasingly practical for non-technical staff to help with DCMS integration.

Open data, being able to access the digital content directly, is the minimal acceptable level of openness for a DCMS. A fundamental requirement for management and preservation is the ability to retrieve digital objects in a complete and standard form. If this is not possible, then the digital content is locked into the DCMS implementation forever. Common mechanisms for retrieving digital objects include export, harvest, web services and query languages.

Export and harvest are ways to retrieve the objects and deposit them outside the system. Export is a function of the system that usually uses a proprietary (unique to each system) request syntax and deposit format that operates locally on the server. Harvest is a network service usually using standard syntax and formats. The Open Archives Initiative Protocol for Metadata Harvesting (OAI-PMH) is a harvest interface that is offered by many digital repository systems (see *http://www.openarchives.org*). OAI-PMH uses a simple URL syntax for requests and returns an XML formatted response. However, a basic OAI-PMH response is encoded as simple Dublin Core (*http://dublincore.org*) and as such only provides some metadata. Although useful for many purposes, this does not meet the basic requirement of open data. OAI-PMH can be extended to encode metadata in more complex and complete forms and to include or provide links to the content files.

As noted above, open services imply open data. If the functionality of the system can be accessed directly then it can be used to retrieve digital objects. Web services are open services that use HTTP requests and XML responses. As with any network service, if all content can be retrieved then some authentication and authorisation scheme is needed to ensure that restricted content is not delivered to unauthorised users. This can be tricky in the web environment so a common alternative is to use a non-network service (like export) to meet the basic open data requirement and use web services to provide unrestricted content only.

If the DCMS uses a database to store digital objects then the database system's query language can often be used to provide open data access. This depends on the database being open or directly accessible without going through the DCMS interfaces and using a published schema to structure the data. Most database systems use a standard query language such as SQL for relational databases or XQuery for XML data sources. Some systems keep metadata and content files in different storage systems, such as a relational database for the metadata and an asset store for the files, and retrieving complete digital objects requires programming of multiple query languages and recombining or packaging of the results.

Scalability refers to a system's ability to expand to meet growing demand. Growth typically occurs along two axes: size and usage. Growing size can mean more digital collections, larger digital collections, larger digital objects or some combination. End-user access and staff management activities can both contribute to growing usage. It is difficult to predict how much growth will ultimately occur, and as this growth will be over some period of time it is not prudent in any case to build or purchase up front a system to handle the largest size and highest usage anticipated. Ideally, a system should be procured that meets modest requirements and that can be upgraded, or scaled up, to meet demands as they grow. This scalability refers to the entire system: hardware, network and the DCMS software. Scaling up hardware (larger storage devices, higher-speed or more processors, more memory) and network (higher bandwidth connections) is well understood by data centre staff; the real issue is how well the DCMS software is able to take advantage of the scaled up systems.

Reliability is a measure of how often a system fails or produces some other kind of error. It is difficult to evaluate by reviewing the system architecture and other materials describing the DCMS components, although one feature to look for is any kind of redundancy, such as mirrored disks in a storage system that can preserve data when a disk crashes. Redundancy can also be applied to other hardware components such as server clusters and network data paths. Better software reliability is often the result of vendor or development community quality assurance (i.e. testing) standards. Perhaps surprisingly, open source software may have an edge here compared with commercial development. Raymond (1999) suggests that the high degree of peer review and user involvement often found in open source software projects contributes to a high level of quality and reliability.

Flexibility refers to the ability to make the system support different ways of using it. It is difficult, if not impossible, to anticipate all the ways in which a system will be used and how the environment in which it is used will change. A flexible system can evolve as requirements and technology change. An open architecture as described above, particularly the availability of APIs, plug-ins and other open services, can enhance the flexibility of a system. Good system design, in particular the separation of the user interface from the business logic of an application, can also contribute to the flexibility.

For example, if webpages are created from HTML templates then staff can customise much of the look and feel. Macros are another mechanism for customising user interfaces. These are display elements that are used in web publishing systems to control the appearance of the page based on the specific data being displayed. They can be very powerful but generally use a proprietary or non-standard syntax. Cascading style sheets are a standard way to control the formatting of HTML pages and provide very powerful customisation tools. Some publishing systems produce XML, which can be processed by XML style sheets (using XSL, another standard) to transform into virtually any kind of output. This is particularly flexible because the custom XSL transformation can target end users with HTML and other services with XML.

Configuration files govern much of the customisation possible in a system. Configuration variables control aspects of the behaviour of the system, such as what metadata to index, what plug-ins to load, and so on. In general, the more behaviours that are controlled by configuration files, the more flexible the system. Configuration variables that can be uniquely specified for different digital collections provide even more flexibility. However, this flexibility can increase the complexity and difficulty with which a system can be deployed. Systems should provide many configuration variables but structure them in logical ways to make them easier to find and customise, and provide reasonable default values for out-of-the-box deployment. A web interface for administration of configuration files can also make the options easier to customise.

Language or locale files represent a kind of configuration file that deserves special mention. These files contain text fragments that are referenced in the code or templates and allow a system to support a user interface in multiple languages. The most flexible systems make it easy to translate and install additional language files. The system also needs to provide an end-user customisation or personalisation page to select the preferred language. Personal preferences for other aspects of the user interface, such as colours and text size, should also be configurable by the end user. Some systems provide a mechanism to create 'skins' or themes that can be selected by the end user to govern the look and feel.

The *platform* is the last aspect of technology that we will consider. This refers to the hardware and software required to host the DCMS components. Obviously, compatibility with the existing IT infrastructure is required. But the technical analysis should go further and examine how well the platform supports the openness, scalability, flexibility and reliability of the overall system.

The network platform is critical for a DCMS, as the system must support multiple users in distributed locations. The internet is the most ubiquitous network platform and the DCMS should support the basic internet protocols. This means that the software components are distributed and act as clients (transmitting requests) or servers (receiving requests and transmitting responses) or both (e.g. peer-to-peer systems). The most flexibility and openness is gained by using web protocols. If the standard web transport protocol (HTTP), identification scheme (URL) and data formats (HTML, XML, JPEG, etc.) are used for client–server interaction then commodity software components, such as a web browser and server, can be used for the software platform. This greatly simplifies deployment because the software platform is freely available and can run on a variety of hardware platforms. More restrictive platform requirements may be acceptable for staff client and server components because they can be controlled more easily than end-user client platforms. However, the functionality supported by those platforms should justify the increased complexity, administrative burden and cost required.

Storage repository

The repository is the heart of the DCMS. It provides storage for the digital objects and is the basis for management and preservation services. Conceptually, as illustrated in Figure 9.2, the repository is in the middle of the production chain, receiving content from the production services and providing content to the dissemination services and, ultimately, the content consumers.

The repository provides multiple levels of storage services. At the most basic level are the physical requirements for storing data on an electronic medium such as a hard drive or optical disc. This includes the method used for storing and organising the data on the medium, such as the disk file system. The file system provides a means for locating and finding computer files and the data they contain.

Access, management and preservation services are built on the basic storage services to provide storage repository implementation. The simplest implementation consists of files that contain the digital content and metadata. A hierarchical directory structure and strict naming convention can organise the files into digital objects and collections. File system commands can be used for browsing and searching the collection, or for creating scripts to deploy a more advanced access services.

However, as more and different kinds of content are put in the repository, organisation based on the file system begins to break down. Error-prone manual processes are required to name and place digital object files in the file system. Naming conventions need to be revised and extended as different kinds of files are included. In addition, search and browse operations take longer and longer to complete. For larger

Figure 9.2   A repository in the digital collection production chain

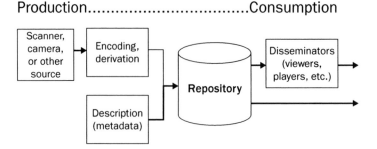

repositories, a database is needed to organise the data and provide reasonable access performance. The database may include the digital content or may just be used to organise the data and contain pointers to the content on the file system. Often a hybrid approach is used, with the files stored in the file system, usually in a 'dark' data store that is only accessible through the repository services, and the descriptive and file metadata stored in the database.

The database also facilitates higher-level repository services for management, administration and preservation. These include facilities to assure data integrity, migrate to new storage media, globally update metadata, and control access. As Kahn and Wilensky (1995) note in their seminal work on repository architecture, the repository's purpose is to provide 'a large and extensible class of distributed digital information services'. They describe access, deposit and naming services built on a network-accessible storage system. Although they specify the data structure and attributes of the digital objects that are stored in the repository, the services are not dependent on or aware of the actual contents of digital objects. By treating stored digital objects as opaque containers, the content of which cannot be seen or utilised, repository services are more easily extended to a wide variety of content.

Storage requirements

The cost per megabyte of hard-drive storage has dropped dramatically over the last decade, and this has provided a huge benefit to repositories of all kinds. Low-cost storage allows for redundancy, which is the best way to ensure the reliability and preservation of electronic data.

Early digitisation projects archived content on optical discs, such as CD-ROM and, later, DVD. However, the lifetime of optical media is variable, depending on factors such as the quality of the media, storage conditions and usage patterns. Storing multiple copies on inexpensive disks that are continually monitored and checked for errors, and migrated to new disks as computer systems evolve, provides much more predictable reliability.

Data storage reliability is a problem that is well understood and various schemes have been developed to address it. Most rely on some form of redundant arrays of inexpensive disks (RAID). RAID can be used to increase data reliability through redundancy. It can also be used for greater input/output performance and larger disk volume size. For reliability, mirroring and data parity calculation allow for the loss of one or more disks in an array without any loss of data.

Arrays also typically support 'hot spares', pre-installed disks that are used to automatically replace a failed drive immediately upon detection of the failure. RAID can have hardware (i.e. a disk controller) and software implementations. Often both are used for the best performance and reliability. For example, the disk controller may implement RAID 5 (striped set with distributed parity) for maximum performance while RAID 1 (mirroring) might be implemented by volume manager software for the greatest flexibility in volume configuration and manipulation.

Another computing development that has made disk arrays more attractive for repository implementations is networked storage. Various mechanisms have been developed to allow the data store to be accessible to multiple hosts. A storage area network (SAN) provides a virtual storage pool that can be partitioned in various ways and mounted by any hosts on the network as if the storage were locally attached. Newer disk access protocols that operate on an ordinary data network, such as NAS and iSCSI (Savyak, 2002) make SAN functionality available at a lower cost and complexity level. Network file systems, such as NFS or SMB (i.e. Windows shares), allow data stores to be mounted by multiple hosts simultaneously. Grid computing research is providing technology for situations where very large data stores need to be distributed across many storage systems. For example, the SDSC Storage Resource Broker (SRB) supports shared collections that can be distributed across multiple organisations and heterogeneous storage systems (see *http://www.sdsc.edu/srb*).

Repositories do not typically provide the storage system specific services for provisioning storage, managing storage devices and migrating between devices. However, a properly architected repository system, with a well-defined storage layer to manage its data store, allows implementations to make use of the appropriate technology to provide storage and to migrate to new storage technologies as requirements dictate.

Backup strategies

A critical storage system service for repositories, as well as any other data management system, is the ability to make backup copies of the data that can be used to restore the original after a data loss event. Data loss can be the result of accidental or intentional deletion, administrative errors or hardware or software failure. The disk array redundancy strategies described above provide some degree of data reliability by guarding against hardware failure. Backup strategies improve on this reliability by maintaining offline copies of important data on separate hardware systems or media. Backups also guard against software and human error by providing a means to roll back a file to a version saved before the deletion or corruption occurred.

Backup strategies have been developed and refined since the early days of computing, resulting in simple reliable procedures that can be used to safeguard data. Historically, backups are written to inexpensive removable media such as tape or optical disc. Although these have limited lifetime and uncertain error rates, the backups are regularly refreshed to get the latest data and ensure the media are error-free. A typical refresh strategy is to backup every file that was modified each night (an incremental backup) and backup every file (a full backup) on a weekly or monthly basis. These backups are usually managed by the enterprise rather than a specific application such as a repository or database. Backup software to schedule and manage backups and recovery range from simple disk copy scripts to distributed systems for scheduling, compressing, encrypting and staging backups for an entire organisation.

The low cost of disks has increased the popularity of disk backups, where the incremental and full backups are written to a separate file system managed by the backup software. This has the advantage of increased performance, which can make a significant difference when backing up hundreds of gigabytes of image files, for example. However, the old strategies have an important benefit: as the tape or optical disc is removable, the backup can be stored offsite and assist in recovery in the case of a fire, flood or other disaster. Even if disk backups are performed on a routine basis, it is a good idea to periodically perform a full backup to some kind of removable media for offsite storage.

A database-driven repository implementation requires a backup strategy that takes care to keep the copies of the database and data store synchronised. Most database systems need to be shutdown or dumped to a special file for backup. The database management system is constantly writing, caching and indexing the data, and if a snapshot is taken while it is in the middle of an operation the data copy may be corrupted. If RAID mirroring is used for storage, then a clean snapshot can be made with minimal downtime by shutting down the database, splitting the mirrors, and using one mirror to backup the data while the database system is brought back up on the other mirrors. Once the backup is complete, the split mirror can be resynchronised with the others.

If the database is managing the identity and location of files in the data store, the database snapshot should be taken simultaneously with the backup copy of the data store. The split mirror strategy can be employed on the data store at the same time that the database management system is brought down to split its mirror. However, this may not be practical for very large data stores. If the repository system can be put in read-only mode to prevent updates, then the data store backup can be taken while no files in the data store are added, changed or removed.

Managing digital content

The management of digital objects and collections does not stop once they are stored in the repository. Repository services support the ongoing administration, maintenance and preservation activities of digital collection management, as well as providing access to the content. Below we explore some of these services as they might be used on an example digital object.

A digital object is stored in the repository immediately or soon after it is created. The repository system provides an ingest or submission service for receiving the digital files and some metadata, assigning an identifier to the digital object that can be used for access, and putting it in a collection. Typically, some technical and administrative metadata are automatically generated when the object is ingested, such as file types and sizes, ingestion date, and so on.

After ingestion, the object may be enhanced or modified by repository update services. In some workflows, the object is submitted to the repository with minimal metadata by the digitisation technician and then later enhanced with descriptive cataloguing by a metadata specialist. Update services can also be used to add or replace content files. For larger collections it is useful to have some kind of global update functionality to add or change a metadata element for an entire collection or selectively (e.g. based on an existing value). Other services to maintain metadata might include definition of metadata schemas and controlled vocabularies. These definitions can then be used to validate an object's descriptive information and generate reports on metadata in the repository.

The digital object must be accessible as soon as it is ingested into the repository. Access services include searching, browsing, dissemination and harvesting. The repository provides management services for defining what metadata elements or content (e.g. full text) are indexed for searching and browsing. The indexes may be automatically updated when objects are ingested or rebuilt by a periodic batch process.

Dissemination services provide all or part of the digital object in response to a network request. Dissemination may be provided through a software application to implement a specific object behaviour, such as 'page turning' to create a navigable web document from an object consisting of multiple image files. Advanced repositories provide a means for binding objects to disseminator programs. Alternatively, the disseminator call can be encoded in the object's structural metadata.

Access services support both administrative access for collection management and end-user access for publication of an object or collection. Publication can occur in multiple contexts by a variety of means. The repository itself may provide a publication service, but it should also provide a service to export the objects for an external presentation or publication system. In addition, the repository should provide a basic export service to facilitate the eventual migration of the content to another repository. Exported digital objects should include all the object components in a file system or data structure from which they can be automatically packaged for submission to the new repository.

OAI-PMH is a network standard for retrieving the metadata for a collection or object from a repository. OAI-PMH can be used to identify the objects that have been added or modified since a specified date, making it a useful protocol for keeping an external publication system synchronised with the repository. OAI-based harvest services typically export just the metadata, not the content files. The metadata includes, of course, an identifier, which can be used to create a link or reference to the digital object in another publication system. However, that link is dependent on the repository and may break if the repository system is modified or the collection is moved to a different repository. It also may not provide a means for linking to specific parts or behaviours of the object. Including disseminator calls in the metadata is a more durable and flexible way to link to the content.

A repository must provide security services in order to support update and access. Access to update services should be limited to authorised collection managers. Access control may be required on particular collections or objects due to licence or copyright restrictions. In addition, collection managers may want to control access to particular parts of a digital object, such as the high-resolution master image files. This implies that the repository needs to provide services for creating and managing users, authorising them for particular roles and collections, and applying access policies to digital objects. A default policy for a collection might be applied to a digital object when it is submitted to the repository, and access control services would provide the ability to modify the authorisation policy for special circumstances.

Preserving digital content

Digital preservation is a commitment to keep digital information accessible over a very long period of time. A repository cannot itself provide digital preservation, because the threats to data preservation, particularly technological change and obsolescence, apply to the repository environment itself. Thus a digital preservation system is not a technology but a system of processes and tools to implement those processes. Hardware (such as storage devices) and software (such as the repository) are components in the system which are replaced as they become obsolete or fail, just as digital content is migrated to new formats and software environments as existing ones age.

Given the rapid pace of technological change and the ephemeral nature of electronic information, the requirement to preserve digital content forever presents a paradox. There is simply no way to predict what processes and repository services will be required to preserve digital collections for hundreds or thousands of years, much less predict what it would cost. Rusbridge proposes a more practical approach that recognises that the repository itself will have a relatively short lifespan:

> It seems to me that it makes more sense for most of us to view digital preservation as a series of holding positions, or perhaps as a relay. Make your dispositions on the basis of the timescale you can foresee and for which you have funding. Preserve your objects to the best of your ability, and hand them on to your successor in good order at the end of your lap of the relay. In good order here means that the digital objects are intact, and that you have sufficient metadata and documentation to be able to demonstrate authenticity, provenance, and to give future users a good chance to access or use those digital objects. (Rusbridge, 2006)

The repository, then, should provide tools to ensure that digital objects are 'in good order', and to transfer or migrate them to the next generation. The repository tools can address near-term predictable threats, such as data loss or corruption and hardware or software failure, rather than attempt to handle an infinite range of long-term risks.

Data is vulnerable to a variety of human and system errors, but lost data can be easily recovered if adequate backup strategies have been implemented. If the loss is complete and catastrophic then the event is obvious and disaster recovery procedures can be implemented to restore the repository. However, some content may not be accessed frequently and the partial loss of a few objects or parts of an object may not be noticed until long after the pre-loss backup media has expired and been replaced with backups also missing the content. The repository needs to provide an audit service to periodically check the asset store and database to ensure that all digital objects are complete and intact.

In some cases, the data may become corrupted or inconsistent, rather than lost as such. This can be the result of media failure, a software defect, or inadvertent or intentional human intervention. As with data loss, the repository needs to provide tools to detect corruption of the digital content. This is typically done with some kind of fixity information, such as a checksum that is uniquely calculated for any stream of data. The checksum is calculated and saved when the content is ingested and then periodically recalculated for every data file and compared with the saved checksums.

Of course, there are legitimate reasons to change digital content and the saved checksum for data should be recalculated when the change is submitted. Provenance information, the documentation of the history of the digital content, should also be recorded whenever legitimate changes occur, as well as when the object was originally ingested. Provenance documentation includes a description of the data ingested or updated (e.g. file name and size), the date it occurred and the name of the person or process responsible. The audit process, then, identifies any changes to the data that were not documented, and can trigger the data recovery process.

Most discussions of digital preservation systems focus on migration as the primary strategy. For example, the Open Archival Information System (OAIS) reference model, which has defined the requirements of digital preservation since it became an ISO standard in 2003, states: 'No matter how well an OAIS maintains its current holdings, it will eventually need to migrate much of its holdings to different media and/or to a different hardware or software environment to keep them accessible' (ISO, 2003). Properly designed storage infrastructure for a repository will take care of routine migration and replication to different media through, for example, backup strategies and RAID deployments. Migration to new formats may be motivated by standardisation and improved technology as well as software obsolescence. The repository need not provide specific migration tools, as that might limit the kinds of format migrations that can be done, but should provide hooks that allow migration tools to copy digital files easily and submit reformatted versions back into the repository.

Migration to new software environments presents a more difficult problem. This also might be motivated more by the features or economy of a new environment than the obsolescence of the old one. Rather than predict and plan for the new environment or systems, a repository implementation should include an exit strategy for getting all the content out of the system, 'in good order' as Rusbridge puts it, so it can be handed off to whatever new environment is implemented.

Usually some digital objects are migrated into the repository when it is first implemented and this process can inform the exit strategy. As discussed in Chapter 4, content models define digital object structure and behaviour. They can be used to govern the creation of digital objects so existing tools for archiving and disseminating the content can be applied to them. When migrating digital objects to a new repository environment, it helps to create a digital object model that is an abstraction of the specific content models for each kind of object. This abstract model documents the structure of the objects in the collections independently of any repository implementation, making it more likely that the objects can be used in the future. In addition, it can be mapped to the data model of the new repository to aid in the migration process.

Digital collections management system software

Digital library software, content management systems and digital asset management systems are examples of integrated software packages that support some aspects of digital collections creation and management. But few provide all the features required of a DCMS, and those that do come with the high cost of ownership and steep learning curve you might expect from such a comprehensive product. In addition, software packages that attempt to include all the features and functions required to build and manage digital collections are usually not very flexible and may not provide the best features for creating, managing and publishing all kinds of digital content.

Implementation of a DCMS typically involves the integration and recombination of distinct programs for digital object creation and workflow, repository storage and services, and collection presentation and publication. The repository, as the central component of a DCMS, is the point where most of this integration occurs and must, therefore, have open interfaces for getting content in and out of the repository. For example, it might provide a web service for ingesting a digital object from the external workflow application that created it. Then, even if the repository is part of a specific kind of content or data management system, it can be adapted for digital collections management.

There are also several repository systems that are designed primarily for electronic documents, journals or other kinds of digital collections managed by libraries, museums and other cultural and research organisations. The Open Society Institute maintains a guide, last updated in 2004, to open source software to help organisations select systems to support institutional repositories of scholarly material (Open Society Institute, 2004). While many of those systems are oriented toward archiving various kinds of text documents, they are, to varying degrees, capable of storing and delivering different kinds of digital media. They are generally based on file systems, which treat all media types as generic streams of bits, and web servers, which are designed to deliver a number of media types, such as images, documents, audio, video and others that are supported by browsers or freely available viewers and players. For example, DSpace (*http://www.dspace.org*), an open source digital asset management system for research materials and publications, provides registries for defining new media types and metadata schemas.

There are a few software systems discussed in the Open Society Institute guide that provide a platform or set of tools for creating a repository. These provide additional flexibility for supporting different media types, metadata schemas and collections management workflows, although more effort may be required to build or integrate specialised workflow management, discovery and delivery services on the repository framework. For example, the Fedora digital repository system (*http://www.fedora-commons.org*) provides little in the way of user interfaces but includes web services interfaces for a management API and an access API. These interfaces can be used by a variety of tools to submit, manage and retrieve content. The repository platform itself provides only basic ingestion and management tools but there is a large community of institutions using Fedora to manage all types of data and information. Many of those institutions are sharing their tools (see *http://www.fedora.info/wiki/index.php/Fedora_Tools*). There are also a few library systems vendors providing tools and support for Fedora-based repositories.

Commercial digital collections systems tend to offer end-to-end solutions addressing all the management requirements for digital object production, archival and delivery. As long as the supported media types, metadata schemas and workflow processes are a good match for the organisational requirements, a commercial solution can provide a relatively quick and easy way to implement a DCMS. For example, CONTENTdm (*http://www.oclc.org/contentdm*), originally developed at the University of Washington and now provided by OCLC, is designed to present primarily visual material on the web. It can, however, be used for other media types, although with fewer features to support their creation and presentation. DigiTool (*http://www.exlibris-usa.com/category/DigiToolOverview*), from ExLibris, is an end-to-end solution that focuses on both digital collections (again, primarily but not exclusively visual material) and scholarly publications (primarily textual material).

End-to-end solutions, while expedient in the short term, may increase longer-term preservation risk. Rosenthal and colleagues at Stanford University have identified some general strategies for preservation that should be considered when evaluating DCMS software. They note the importance of transparency and diversity to enable auditing and migration of content and incremental evolution and enhancement of services. In particular, closed or proprietary formats, protocols and interfaces '[render] the preserved information hostage to the vendor's survival and [are] hard to justify' (Rosenthal, et al., 2005).

There is a wide range of software packages from which DCMS software components may be chosen and the list continues to grow, so it is not possible to describe them all. Table 9.1, however, provides a comparison of a sample in terms of how the vendor and development community define the product and the software functionality focus.

Case study: the DCPC digital collections management system

The DCPC digital collections management system consists of web applications for digital object creation and workflow (such as DCEditor, described in the Chapter 6 case study), a DSpace repository, a digital collections website (built with Greenstone Digital Library Software) and various disseminator programs for viewing and navigating through complex digital objects. DSpace includes a simple plug-in mechanism for customising and extending the repository system. We created plug-in Java classes that implement specific methods for accessing the repository API to create a web services interface for ingesting, modifying or retrieving archived content (Gourley, 2007). We used this interface to integrate the DCPC digital object creation and dissemination tools with DSpace for our digital collections management system.

DSpace has a well-defined storage layer encapsulating an asset store for storing content in a file system and a relational database for storing

Table 9.1   Example software packages with DCMS functionality

Name	Open source or commercial	Vendor definition	Main focus
CONTENTdm	C	Digital collection management package	Creating and organising collections Searching and accessing collections Managing collections
DigiTool	C	Digital asset management	Managing and providing access to digital resources Creating and managing institutional repositories with ease
DSpace	O	Digital repository system	Repositories at an institutional level Self-deposit of digital assets by faculty End-user interface for depositors Assets made available for searching and browsing Data retrievable many years in the future Institutional commitment to ensure the continued availability of certain named formats (Witten et al., 2005)
EPrints	O	Platform for building high-quality, high value repositories	Metadata and full-text searching Subscriptions (alerting service) Exporting metadata as XML Batch imports via XML OAI-compliant Multilingual support via Unicode Command line tools (Jayakanth, 2007)
Fedora*	O	Digital object repository management system	Flexible digital object model Content versioning XML ingest and export XML storage Object-to-object relationships Access control and authentication

Table 9.1 Example software packages with DCMS functionality (*Cont'd*)

Name	Open source or commercial	Vendor definition	Main focus
			Simple search RDF-based resource index OAI metadata harvesting provider Migration utility Batch utility Reporting utility
Greenstone	O	Digital library software	Design and construction of collections Distribution on the web and/or removable media Customised structure depending on available metadata End-user collection-building interface for librarians Reader and librarian interfaces in many languages Multiplatform operation (Witten et al., 2005)
Insight Software[†]	C	Software for digital collections	Working with visual collections Building visual collections quickly and easily Managing and cataloguing visual collections Sharing collections and accessing others Centralising and securing visual resources

O, open source; c, commercial
[*]See *http://www.fedora.info/download/2.0/userdocs/server/features/features.html*
[†]See *http://www.lunaimaging.com/insight/index.html*

metadata and asset store management information (Tansley et al., 2003). The asset store is opaque, in the sense that files and directories are given random names and access is completely controlled by the repository. Different implementations can be used in the storage layer without affecting other parts of the system. For example, SRB can replace the file

Figure 9.3   The DCPC digital collections management system

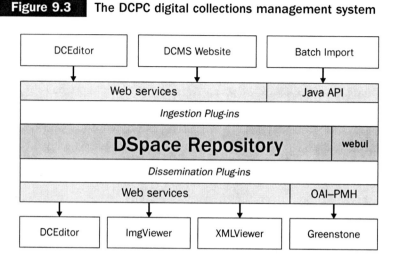

system for an asset store. The database stores all information about the organisation of the asset store, metadata about the content, and user authorisation and authentication. Metadata includes automatically generated fixity and provenance information that can be used in independent audit processes. Every night, repository updates are disabled while we dump the database and perform an incremental backup on the file system. On a quarterly schedule, the entire asset store and database are backed up to tapes, which are transferred to a remote location for storage. Figure 9.3 illustrates the DCPC digital collections management system implementation.

Repository data modelling

DSpace has a specific data model for organising information in the repository. The repository is divided into *communities*, which contain *collections*, each of which contains *items*, which are the basic archival elements of the repository. Items include metadata records and bundles of bitstreams, the latter being ordinary computer files (Tansley et al., 2003). Communities, collections and items are given unique identifiers called *handles*, based on the Corporation for National Research Initiatives' Handle System (*http://www.handle.net*). Before setting up the repository, we needed to create a model for the DCPC collections and objects that could be mapped to the DSpace data model. At the higher levels, there are obvious correlations between the DCPC content and the

DSpace model: communities correspond to the consortium libraries, digital collections are groupings of related content in both models, and DSpace items correspond to our digital objects.

To support complex digital objects, we defined an abstract digital object model that consists of a unique persistent identifier and various kinds of data. Data is partitioned into metadata and content classes. Multiple metadata classes with distinct schemas can be used to represent different kinds of metadata (descriptive, administrative, and so on). Qualified Dublin Core is DSpace's native metadata format, which can be extended with additional qualifiers. DSpace also supports different metadata schemas that can be registered in the system by specifying their elements and qualifiers. These item metadata records are used to implement the metadata classes in our digital object model.

Content classes contain the individual components of the digital object, and are given specific types to indicate the kind of digital representation or derivation contained in that class, such as display or thumbnail image files. A dissemination content class, with references to external viewers or players for the object, contains static bindings of the object to the disseminator programs. Components contain or reference digital content files and are typed and sequenced. These content classes map naturally to DSpace bundles. Components that are content files similarly map to DSpace bitstreams. Reference components need a bitstream representation in DSpace, which we implement with XHTML meta refresh files that can be parsed as XML to dereference the component link, or processed as a URL redirect by most web browsers.

The abstract model wraps the content into a manifest that exposes individual classes and components along with their structural metadata. There is no obvious element in the DSpace data model that corresponds to our manifest. Extended metadata schemas in DSpace are 'flat' and cannot express the hierarchy needed for structural metadata. In addition, there is no persistent identifier assigned to individual bitstreams that can be used to construct a URL to access that content file. As such, we chose to implement the manifest as a separate bitstream that is stored in a special bundle. The manifest file includes the item handle and lists the contents of each item bundle, including links to access each bitstream, and type and sequence metadata. DIDL is used to encode the manifest as it provides a simple and flexible way to describe structure that is not constrained by the requirements of any particular data model. The DSpace data model mapping is illustrated in Figure 9.4.

Figure 9.4 DSpace data model mapping

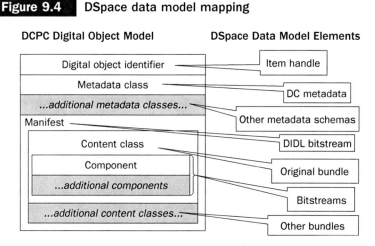

DCPC Digital Object Model   DSpace Data Model Elements

Digital object submission and dissemination

DIDL is also used to package digital objects for submission and dissemination. On submission, a DIDL package with a digital object's metadata and pointers to the associated image files can be created by the DCEditor or by a batch process, depending on the DCPC's workflow requirements for that collection. The particular makeup of the package, such as which content classes are included and which disseminator programs are linked, is based on the content model for the new digital object. For example, a serial article might include sequenced display-resolution images for each page and the URL to invoke the page turning disseminator application. After a DIDL package representing a digital object is created, DCPC staff can click on the 'submit' button to upload it to the repository submission plug-in. The plug-in reads the package and invokes the DSpace API methods to create the metadata records, ingest the content files and assign the item handle. The plug-in then creates and ingests the manifest.

A DIDL package that contains descriptive and structural metadata is created by the dissemination plug-in. The DCEditor invokes that plug-in to export a digital object from the repository for enhancement, correction and other modification. Metadata and content files can be modified in the editor and then processed by the submission plug-in much like new objects. If an image file needs to be replaced, the new one can be uploaded into the editor with the same name as the old one and the submission plug-in will move the old one to a 'versioning' bundle and replace it with the new one in the original bundle. The submission plug-in will also record all changes to bitstreams and bundles as provenance metadata in the repository database.

A nightly process uses DSpace's OAI-PMH interface to check whether any content in each collection has been created or modified and, if changes have been made, export DIDL packages for all items in the collection. Those packages are then imported into Greenstone and the collection is rebuilt to update the collection website. Digital collections can also be harvested from the repository and imported into Greenstone by collection managers to test configuration or data changes. When the harvested digital objects are imported, links to the components of our digital object model, whether content files or disseminators, are copied to metadata elements in the Greenstone collection. This allows the file and disseminator links to be invoked from the Greenstone website.

Complex digital objects and functional behaviours are implemented by structuring the digital objects in our repository according to specific data and content models. DSpace provides implicit support through its extensible metadata schemas and bitstream data types, but digital object creation and dissemination are not dependent on this particular repository implementation in the DCMS.

As technology and processes evolve, components of the DCMS can be modified or replaced independently. For example, we are not locked into one repository with support for a specific implementation of complex object structures or behaviours. With appropriate data modelling we can migrate the digital collections to a new repository while reusing the other components of the DCMS. Similarly, ingestion and dissemination tools can be added without affecting the repository implementation or the other parts of the system.

10

Selecting software and hardware for digital collections management systems

As discussed in Chapter 9, a digital collections management system (DCMS) includes software and hardware that support the digital content creation, storage, management, presentation and preservation functions required for digital collections management. As the selection of software and hardware both undertake similar processes, we will discuss the general process and point out differences when needed.

Although a variety of software programs perform many of those functions required by a DCMS, choosing a package that will best meet the needs of an organisation and its digitisation projects is challenging. The selection process should involve representatives from all the groups that have a stake in the organisation's digitisation projects. The stakeholders may include content providers such as special collections, archives and other library departments, metadata providers such as cataloguers and other metadata specialists, information technology staff such as programmers and web designers, and management staff such as the project manager and library director. Target users of the digital collections are also important stakeholders in the projects. A team of representatives from the stakeholders should be responsible for gathering ideas, suggestions and requirements from all stakeholders and for undertaking the systems selection process.

The selection process includes these four steps:

1. identify organisational requirements and resources;
2. develop selection criteria;
3. research available systems and equipment;
4. evaluate candidates.

Figure 10.1 Process of selecting software and hardware

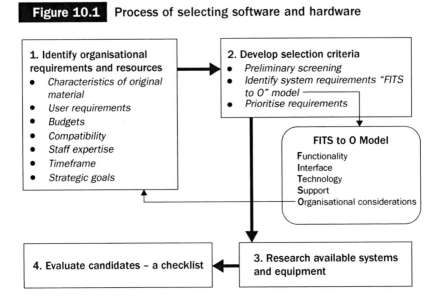

Figure 10.1 illustrates the process and details of each step, as well as the 'FITS to O' model we are going to introduce in this chapter.

Identify organisational requirements and resources

Different libraries have different organisational structures, strategic goals and technical infrastructures, as well as different financial and human resources. For example, the technical expertise that is available to support and perhaps develop DCMS software varies from library to library. In addition, different digitisation projects have different goals, purposes and scopes. A single library or a department of a library may initiate some small-scale projects. Other digitisation projects may be collaborative between several libraries and institutions, or even all the libraries in a consortium or state system such as Connecticut History Online (*http://www.cthistoryonline.org/cdm-cho/index.html*) or the California Digital Library (*http://www.cdlib.org*). There are regional and nationwide digitisation projects that are very large-scale, such as the Collaborative Digitization Program (*http://www.cdpheritage.org/index.html*) that includes ten western states and the National Science Digital Library (*http://nsdl.org*). Consequently, the specific requirements are different from project to project, depending on the library or organisations that are involved. Identifying these organisational requirements and resources is a crucial first step in the selection of hardware and software to support digitisation and digital collections management.

Organisational requirements can be categorised by several aspects, described in the following sections.

Characteristics of original material

It is very important to take the time to identify and analyse the potential original material for digitisation and the structure of the contents. The original materials for digital imaging can be divided into several types and each type may require the software and hardware to offer different features and functions.

- *Single page images.* These are objects that contain only one image. Examples include photographs (prints, negatives or slides), postcards, posters and drawings. The requirements for metadata creation and online display for single page images are straightforward: one metadata record is required for each individual image and the image can be displayed directly in a web browser, either by itself or within an HTML page.

- *Multi-page images.* By this we mean one item that contains potentially several related and sequenced images. Examples include letters, manuscripts, books, magazines, newspapers and scrapbooks. This type of material requires software support to assemble the images and metadata record into one digital object. The presentation requires some mechanism to link the images together in sequence. This can be coded by hand in HTML but software that can automatically generate the 'page-turning' links is required when creating more than just a handful of multi-page image objects. If the original material is bound, such as with books and magazines, special digitisation equipment, such as an overhead book scanner or a digital camera, is required to create good-quality images.

- *Oversize materials.* These include large-format books, newspapers, maps, and so on. Effective online display of oversize materials requires presentation software with zooming and panning features. Typical inexpensive production scanners cannot scan anything larger than about 12×17 inches (30×43 cm), so digitising oversize materials requires more expensive specialised equipment such as a large-format scanner or a digital camera.

- *Text-based materials.* These may include books, magazines and newspapers that are to be converted into full-text searchable documents. Optical character recognition (OCR) software is required to digitise the full-text (as opposed to just taking a picture of it). OCR software analyses the character shapes in an image to generate digital text that can be embedded in documents (e.g. in PDF or Word format). The text can also be indexed to support full-text searching capability in the digital collection presentation.

- *Slides, negatives and 35-mm film strips, etc.* These materials require special scanners with relatively high scanning resolution although software requirements may be the same as the relevant category above.

In addition to material types, the structure of the contents and relationships between digital objects and collections also need to be considered. For example, a photograph of a reporter interviewing a musician may have an associated sound recording, which is catalogued separately in another collection. The software must have the ability to link between the two objects.

Identifying the types in the original collections enables one to make sound decisions regarding hardware and software selection.

User requirements

The potential users of a digital collection include researchers, educators, students, organisation staff and the general public. These can be divided into two groups: staff users and target users.

Staff users are librarians, archivists and curators of the special collections who provide the contents for digitising. It is important to understand why they selected the material for digitisation and how they expect to use the digital collection. Do they want to use the digital collection as a means of preservation, access, or as an inventory tool? How do they want to search the collection? How do they want to present the collection to the target user groups? Do any access restrictions need to be placed on the digital content? If the project is a collaboration between several institutions, the requirements of the staff users at each individual institution also need to be considered. Do they want to brand each individual collection? Do they want to browse collections by institution? Do they want to search across collections? These questions need to be answered in order to identify the staff user needs.

Target users can include anyone who has access to the internet. Usually, a focused audience is first defined when planning a digitisation project. This will help in the process of selecting software. For example, if the target audiences are children in elementary schools, the presentation requirements might include simple navigation, highly-visual display and animated objects. If the target audience includes professional artists and fine-arts students, the requirements might include image manipulation tools for cropping, rotating, polishing and enhancing pictures, and features such as creating and exporting dynamic presentations, viewing three-dimensional objects, and creating annotations and linking.

User requirements should be considered open-ended. That is, after carefully analysing the needs of the staff and target users, always assume that additional uses and audiences will be discovered and need to be accommodated. The collection and/or digital objects in the collection should be easily reused for other projects and linked to other collections or websites. The construction of the objects and collection should not restrict such reuse and repurposing. This means that the DCMS should be open in the sense that the digital objects can be accessed and exported for use in different and possibly unanticipated environments.

Budgets

The price of digitisation includes many hidden and ongoing costs. The software and hardware purchase is only a small portion of the overall budget for a digitisation project. The purchase cost should be taken into consideration first, but the ongoing costs to maintain and administer those systems need to be considered in the total cost of ownership. In many cases there is a trade-off between initial spending and long-term expenditure. For example, free open source software has no initial cost but may require skilled (and expensive) technical staff to keep it running. If that expertise is not in-house, expenses for consultant help need to be factored into the budget. As another example, a basic flatbed scanner may be selected for its low cost, but with a slower scanning speed it may require more staff time and expenses to operate.

If these hidden costs are exposed and considered with respect to the available resources then the appropriate trade-offs can be made to ensure that a project can completed within its budget. If there is no capital budget for expensive equipment to digitise oversize maps in sufficient resolution, perhaps enough operating cash can be found to outsource the digitisation to a service firm that can amortise the capital expense over a large number of projects. If no money can be found to purchase an expensive software tool, perhaps a talented programmer is available to help develop and maintain the functionality in-house.

Compatibility

Selecting hardware and software that are compatible with the existing technology infrastructure is another important consideration. For example, if the organisation uses Windows servers on its network then a digital object repository that only runs on Linux should not be considered. Similarly, a Mac-based metadata editor cannot be considered in an organisation that uses PCs on the desktop. To avoid desktop compatibility problems, look for tools that run on a server and use web browser clients for the user interface. That way, use of the DCMS does not depend on any specific software being installed on the desktop or any specific location, as long as there is a connection to the web.

Server compatibility problems and in-house integration efforts are eased by the use of distributed systems that can run on a variety of servers and communicate via network interfaces. If libraries have (or may acquire) other digital resources, such as e-journals, e-books, etc., they can be more easily integrated with the DCMS if there are open network interfaces for accessing the functionality of each system. For example, a meta-search engine can provide a federated search across all the resources if they support a network search interface like Z39.50 (*http://www.niso .org/standards/resources/Z3950_Resources.html*) or SRU/W (*http://www.loc .gov/standards/sru*).

This openness is extremely important for overcoming a variety of compatibility problems. The DCMS should have open interfaces for importing and exporting collections. If a library has existing digital collections that were built in older systems, the import interface can be used to integrate those collections into the new DCMS. An export interface can be used to copy digital content into specialised applications such as media-streaming servers. These interfaces should use accepted content formats and metadata schemas to minimise the amount of custom programming required to transfer content between systems. As with user requirements, compatibility requirements will continue to evolve and a DCMS that locks the content into a closed environment is doomed to early obsolescence.

Staff expertise

Implementing and managing a DCMS requires a variety of technical expertise. The skills, knowledge, specialties and experiences of project staff play a very important role in the selection of the DCMS software and digitisation equipment. Typically, the more flexible and powerful a software package, the more technical expertise is required to configure and customise it to meet organisational needs. If that expertise is not available then it might be preferable to select an 'out-of-the-box' package that requires little customisation and then adapt workflow to meet its requirements.

Staff expertise in project planning and management is also an important factor in the selection of DCMS software. Experienced digitisation managers can design clever and efficient workflow and procedures that take advantage of the strengths of the software package and avoid some of its weaknesses. Less experienced managers should look for tools that implement and support widely accepted best practices for digitisation.

A final consideration is who will be using and operating the software and hardware systems. Are there any trained staff? Will any dedicated staff need to be trained, or will student workers be used? It may be difficult to train non-professionals to use software that is designed for professional librarians and makes use of a lot of information science jargon.

Timeframe

Some projects, especially grant-funded projects, have specific time constraints. When selecting DCMS components, one must take into consideration the time and effort required to install, configure and test the new system. The learning curves mentioned in the staff expertise requirements take on additional importance when a tight schedule is imposed.

Strategic goals

A library's strategic plan should be consulted in selecting software and hardware. Does the DCMS align with the overall information technology plans? Will it help the library accomplish its strategic initiatives? Is it flexible, advanced and open enough to accommodate rapid developments in technology? In answering these questions it is important to talk to the strategic planners in the organisation, such as the chief information officer and library management team.

Develop selection criteria

The next step in choosing the DCMS software and hardware is to develop specific selection criteria based on the organisational requirements and resources that have been identified.

Preliminary screening

Preliminary screening can help organisations quickly narrow down the scope of the choices by listing the organisational needs and resources and matching them to basic hardware and software requirements. Table 10.1 shows a very simple example of a preliminary screening matrix.

The table shows a planned digitisation project that will consist of 70 per cent photographs, 20 per cent books and a small number of maps. The staff that will be scanning material, editing metadata and constructing digital objects will use PCs running Windows. This is a two-year project with a starting budget of $5,000 for software and hardware. The library wants to build a sustainable digitisation service for the long term.

A quick outline of the organisational needs and resources for software and hardware indicate the preliminary requirements:

- Windows-based client software. This will exclude software for other operating systems such as Linux or Mac.
- The maximum starting budget is $5,000. This will give several options. If open source software is selected, the $5,000 can all be spent on digitisation equipment. If commercial software is preferred, it must share the $5,000 with digitisation equipment. There is at least $2,000 dedicated for ongoing expenses each year. If digitisation equipment for all types of material is unaffordable, some of the oversize or bound material can be sent out for digitisation.
- The display requirements include zooming and panning, and page-turning facilities as there are maps and books that need to be digitised.

Identify system requirements: the 'FITS to O' model

The next step is to identify the system requirements in detail. A list of requirements for the DCMS can grow very large, so it is best to group them into manageable categories. Based on experience and the work of Han (2004) and Goh et al. (2006), we summarised a model called 'FITS to Organisations' or 'FITS to O' for use in identifying system requirements

Table 10.1 A simple example of a preliminary screening matrix

	Description	Software requirements	Digitisation equipment
Types of material	70% photographs	Display thumbnails Display larger images	Flatbed scanner
	20% books	Page turning Full-text searching	Book scanner
	10% maps	Zooming Panning	Large-format scanner or digital camera
User needs	Staff users	Brand each collection Metadata creation Content management	N/A
	Target users	Web interface User-friendly	N/A
Desktop compatibility	100% PCs	Windows XP	PCI hardware (USB or SCSI); Windows-compatible drivers
Timeframe	Two-year project	Must install and use in two months	Used for at least two years
Budget	Max. $5,000 initial costs; $2,000 p.a. operating costs	Max. $3,000 purchase; $500 maintenance p.a.	Max. $2,000 equipment; $1,500 outsourcing p.a.
Expertise	Metadata schemas; XML encoding; Perl scripting	Dublin Core description Open, XML-based APIs	N/A
Strategic goal	Sustain the service	System maintenance and enhancement Data migration	Equipment maintenance and upgrading

p.a., per annum

and selecting and evaluating DCMS components. We also created a checklist for evaluating DCMS that is listed in Appendix A.

'FITS to Organisation' refers to functionality, interface, technology, support and organisational considerations.

Functionality

By functionality we mean how a software/system works, its capabilities, what it allows a user to do and what it can do for a user to support digital collections management.

Although a DCMS differs from a content management system (CMS) in some ways, many concepts in selecting a CMS system can be applied to DCMS selection (see, for example, Robertson, 2002). We divided functionality into five categories:

- content creation;
- content management;
- content discovery;
- content presentation;
- content preservation.

Content creation includes functionality for acquiring and creating digital objects (i.e. digital data and metadata). Considerations for content creation should include:

- Is the system integrated with digitisation hardware?
- What kinds of metadata creation tools does it provide?
- Does it support flexible workflows for creating digital objects?
- Can objects and metadata be imported/exported individually and in bulk?
- What file formats does it support?
- What metadata schemas does it support?
- Can it do file conversions?

Content management addresses features and tools for organising digital objects and collections, managing access control, and producing statistics. Basic questions about content management include:

- How are the collections managed?
- How are the objects organised?
- How can access to collections, items, digital content files and metadata be controlled?
- Are there tools for automating collection creation and building?
- Are there tools for updating, deleting or replacing digital objects, individually or globally?

- Is appropriate provenance documentation saved when items are modified?
- What kinds of statistics can the system supply?

Content discovery refers to the mechanisms that allow end users to find and access digital material of interest. The selection criteria should emphasise:

- What kinds of query features does the system support?
- What options are available for browsing through the content?
- Is it interoperable with other search and discovery systems in the library and the greater community?
- Are metadata and digital content files accessible for future new and unanticipated uses?

Content presentation refers to the functionality that allows end users to view and manipulate the digital content. The selection criteria should ask:

- How does the system deliver content to the end user? (e.g. web, CD-ROM, portable devices)
- What web browsers does it support?
- Are stylesheets and templates used to allow local customisations?
- What functionality is available for viewing, playing or manipulating different media formats?
- Is it extensible, allowing new disseminators to be used for presenting different kinds of digital content?

Content preservation refers to the long-term archival of metadata and content, quality-control measures to ensure integrity, and persistent documentation identification for migration purposes (Hedstrom, 2001). The questions to be answered include:

- Does the system provide persistent identification for objects and collections?
- Does it support multiple redundant copies of data and metadata?
- Are there tools for migrating objects to different storage media and file formats?
- Can the system manage different versions of objects?
- Can it automatically recognise the format of digital content files?

Interface

The interface defines the communication boundary between the software and the user. It is the way software exposes and presents its underlying functionality. It is usually called the 'user interface' or 'look and feel' of the system. Modern software design encourages the separation of the user interface from the functionality (or 'business logic') of an application. Similarly, when evaluating systems like a DCMS, the functionality and the user interface should be evaluated separately.

Perhaps the most critical interface requirement for a DCMS is for it to be user-friendly. By this we mean the ease with which the DCMS can be used to complete a particular task. Different users will be using the DCMS for different tasks. These tasks can be broadly categorised as management tasks performed by various library staff and end-user tasks performed by those in the target audience. Thus, there are two types of interfaces that need to be considered, namely, the staff interface and the end-user interface.

The *staff interface* is for library staff to use to create digital content files and metadata and to manage digital content. Creating and managing digital collections requires a powerful, flexible and user-friendly interface. These requirements are often competing so some balance is required. For example, data entry steps that closely match staff workflow will save time and staff resources and make the operation more efficient, but features to make data entry steps flexible to match different workflows may make the interface more complex and less easy to use. Because of these important considerations, the list of requirements for the staff interface may be very long. The basic questions to ask are:

- Does the system have a web interface or do staff users need to install special client software on their desktop computers to access the system?
- Can multiple staff members use the staff interface at the same time without interfering with each other?
- Does it provide different levels of authorisation for student workers, staff members and administrators?
- What workflows does it support for digitisation and digital object creation?
- What kinds of tools does it provide for metadata entry and modification?

- What kinds of advanced search/browse options does it provide for staff to use?
- Does it have tools for customising the staff and end-user interfaces?
- What tools does it have for creating and building collections?
- Does it provide online help, tutorials and examples?

The *end-user interface* is what the target audience users use to access the digital collections. An end user will use the interface to find information, to retrieve digital objects, to view, play and manipulate multimedia content, and to personalise their preferences. While usability is most critical, the general appearance and attractiveness of the end-user interface are also important. When evaluating an end-user interface, consider these questions:

- Does it provide simple search and advanced search?
- What browse options does it provide?
- What kinds of navigation tools does it have?
- Can the interface be customised by administrator/staff?
- Can the interface be personalised by end users?
- Does it support different languages?
- Does it provide help on search, browse and technical issues?
- Can users send comments, ask questions and report problems?

Technology

As described in Chapter 9, technology refers to the design, architecture and components that make up the management system software package. The software standards, frameworks and application programming interfaces used to design and create the software package can have an enormous effect on the overall flexibility and scalability of the system. However, the technology is difficult to evaluate without detailed examination of the system design by information technology specialists. If this expertise is not available in the library, then the organisation's IT department should be recruited to participate in the evaluation of DCMS technology. In addition, the people that will be managing and administering the computer systems that support the DCMS should be involved in the technology evaluation to ensure that the system meets the organisation's IT infrastructure requirements.

When evaluating technology for a DCMS, the five issues regarding system technology we discussed in the previous chapter should be considered, namely: openness, scalability, reliability, flexibility and platform.

The basic questions regarding *openness* include:

- Does the system support a standard query language for accessing metadata and content?
- Can digital objects be exported and harvested easily?
- Does the system provide web services or other open APIs to access the system functionality?
- Does the system have a mechanism for adding functionality via locally-developed or third-party plug-ins?
- Is the system source code open and available for inspection and modification?

The most effective way to judge the *scalability* is to review deployments of the system at other institutions. Consider these questions when reviewing system deployments:

- What are the largest digital collections it supports?
- Do performance issues arise as collection size increases? It is important to look at both end-user functionality performance (e.g. the time it takes to return search results) and performance of management functions (e.g. the time it takes to index a collection).
- Do performance issues arise as more users access the system?
- Can the system be scaled up (i.e. by adding more processes, memory or storage devices) to address performance issues?
- Can the system be scaled out (i.e. by distributing programs over multiple servers) to address performance issues and improve reliability?

As with scalability, it is best to evaluate *reliability* by surveying institutions that have used or are using the components to learn from their experiences. Ask the system users and administrators questions such as:

- How often do components fail or become unavailable?
- Do any service requests produce incorrect results (e.g. a search query that does not find all matching content)?
- Can data or metadata become corrupted?

Flexibility can be evaluated by asking the questions like:

- Is the system based on an open architecture that supports different ways of configuring and using the system?
- Does the system support different kinds of digital content?
- What kind of tools (e.g. HTML templates, stylesheets, macros, etc.) does this system provide for configuring the system and user interfaces?
- What kinds of attributes can be configured in the configuration files?
- Does the user interface support multiple languages?
- Does the system support preferences that can be customised by individual users?

Questions for evaluating the *platform* include:

- Is it a 'client–server' application?
- What server and desktop operating systems are supported?
- Is it compatible with existing IT infrastructure?
- What are the requirements for client software to access the system?

Support

Support includes various services that the software vendors or developers provide to support users and managers of the software package. Support and services can be divided into four categories:

- purchase/acquisition;
- documentation;
- technical support;
- upgrading.

Purchase/acquisition defines the supports and services for acquiring the DCMS software. Questions to be asked include:

- Is this software downloadable from a website?
- Does it allow full-feature trial or evaluation?
- Does the vendor or developer website provide detailed information about the software?
- Is there a return policy?

Documentation addresses whether the DCMS package includes written instructions, user manuals, etc. and whether it is easy to obtain them.

- Does it include a user manual?
- Does it have a developer's manual?
- Does it contain tutorials and examples?
- Are the manuals available on the web or in printed format?

Technical support is the level of help or service available for resolving problems that occur while configuring and using the DCMS.

- Are any forms of online help available?
- Is there a phone number to call?
- Is there a contact e-mail address?
- Is onsite support available?
- Are there any training classes available?

Upgrading refers to the support and services that are needed to upgrade the software.

- Is there a mechanism for requesting new features?
- Is bug tracking available?
- What skills are required to upgrade a system?
- Are there services available to implement an upgrade?
- What costs are associated with maintenance and upgrading?

Organisational considerations

Functionality, interface, technology and support explain detailed selection criteria for a DCMS software package. In addition to FITS, organisational considerations should play an essential role in the selection process. The organisational needs and resources identified earlier should be assigned weights according to the level of their importance. The weights should be used to weight the total scores of the system requirements. This will be explained in detail later in this chapter.

Prioritise requirements

Prioritisation does not have to be an exhaustive ranking of every requirement. To narrow down the candidates, identify the most important requirements (the 'must-haves'). The most important requirements are those that are critical to success. Without the must-have features, the DCMS cannot meet the basic needs of the organisation. Selection criteria should be developed based on these most critical features.

A checklist in Appendix A provides a long list of requirements for FITS. It can be used to identify the most important features and create a requirements list. As an example, Table 10.2 lists a few categories that

Table 10.2   Shortlist of 'must-have' features

Functionality
  Content creation
    Content acquisition
      Bulk upload content files
      Bulk upload metadata in XML
      Export specified content files
      Export specified metadata
    File formats supported
      TIFF
      JPEG
      PDF
    Metadata creation
      Support qualified Dublin Core descriptive metadata
      Support XML-based hierarchical metadata schemas
      Automatic link associated objects
      Assemble multi-page objects
  Content management
    Objects
      Add/delete objects
      Auto generation of relationships

Interface
  End-user interface
    Search
      Keywords
      Full-text
    Display
      Zooming and panning
    Navigation
      Page turning

Technology
  Operating system
    Windows XP

More …

contain the most important features to meet the requirements for the preliminary screening in Table 10.1. This shortlist will be used for identifying potential candidate systems and components in the next step.

Research available systems and equipment

Once selection criteria are developed and prioritised, it will start to become clear what kind of system is needed. The next step is to identify the software and hardware components that satisfy the criteria.

Very few systems are marketed as digital collections management systems. However, there are some software packages that sound similar but are usually not appropriate for digital collections management. For example, do not confuse a content management system (CMS) with a DCMS. The CMS has a much broader scope and does not provide support for requirements that are unique to digital collections, such as metadata standards and digital preservation. In addition, do not confuse a DCMS with systems that are designed to manage broader or different kinds of collections, such as an integrated library system (typically used to manage print material) or an electronic resource management system (typically used to manage licensed electronic resources).

Perhaps the closest in concept to digital collection management is digital asset management (DAM). But as Dahl et al. (2006) state, 'DAM is not a technology per se; it is a set of policies and social commitments that define purpose, scope and desired outcomes'. They go on to point out that a wide range of DAM software solutions have been developed to address the multifaceted nature of DAM. Digital collections management is one facet and as such a DAM system may support many of the criteria for a DCMS.

As noted above, the DCMS is a collection of components that support all aspects of digital collection management: content creation, management, discovery, presentation and preservation. This makes the investigation of candidate systems more challenging as a variety of products aimed at different business markets may best satisfy different criteria. While some systems may offer more of a solution than others, we do not believe there is any fully integrated system that contains all the software and hardware components required of a DCMS. It is important to compare systems based on the functionality they have in common. Comparing apples with oranges is one of the most common mistakes made during the selection process.

It may be useful to identify a few broad functional areas and evaluate candidate systems within those areas. More than one component may be needed to meet the requirements of a single functional area, and some systems may provide functionality in multiple areas, but this kind of division can make the grouping and comparison of components more manageable by reducing the number of component combinations that are evaluated. Functional areas that we have found useful for system evaluation and comparison are:

- digitisation (equipment and software used to create digital content files);
- digital object creation (software to create and edit digital objects);
- repository (software to support management and preservation);
- publishing (software to support discovery and presentation).

Open source vs. commercial software

Application software comes in variety of forms, including packaged (or 'shrink-wrapped'), domain-specific, shareware and open source. In the digital library domain it is important to understand the differences between commercial domain-specific software and open source software. According to the Open Source Initiative, 'Open source is a development method for software that harnesses the power of distributed peer review and transparency of process' (Open Source Initiative, 2007). The attributes of open source software include: free distribution of software and source code, licences that allow distribution of modifications and derived works, and non-discrimination against persons, groups or fields of endeavour. A commercial company may sell an open source software package for profit; however, the package will include the source code, the use of which is free from most restrictions. Commercial support for open source software may be available for a fee.

Commercial software is sold or licensed by a commercial company or a vendor without the source code and with restrictions on how (if at all) it may be modified and redistributed. Often the licence is for a specific number of instances and additional licences must be purchased to deploy or distribute the software further. New versions or upgrades to the software may require additional fees. Support and maintenance for the software may be part of the package or cost extra.

The availability of the source code in open source software allows anyone to modify and make improvements to it. Even if an organisation does not have the resources or intention of modifying the software, the availability offers important advantages. The modifications and code contributions can come from a diverse talent pool of programmers in the user community. Thus, having been developed by the software users themselves, open source software tends to have more functions than commercial software, where the vendor's priority is in profit generation rather than the needs of users (von Hippel and von Krogh, 2003).

There are no guarantees about the long-term viability of any software application. For commercial applications you should look at the financial strength of the vendor and its history of adapting to changes in technology and the marketplace. Similarly, for open source software, examine the community of users and developers that has formed around the application. Is development spread across a variety of institutions or is it centred at one organisation and focused on their requirements? Are there active mail lists, blogs, wikis and other online systems where users and developers support each other? Do any commercial companies offer support for the application or include the application in their commercial offerings?

In general, open source software requires less investment up front to acquire and deploy, but more resources (such as IT expertise) to configure and manage the systems on an ongoing basis. With open source software there is also less likelihood of being dependent on a single software provider or being trapped into long-term software support contracts, which restrict flexibility in implementation (Surman and Diceman, 2004).

Gathering software and vendor information

Information about the various systems available can be gathered from a variety of sources, for example:

- network with other libraries to learn what equipment and software they use for similar digital collections projects;
- attend conferences and exhibitions to see demonstrations and presentations of software packages;
- ask questions and seek recommendations on relevant e-mail lists and discussion boards;
- search for websites of similar projects and contact the project manager;
- read articles and case studies about digital collections management activities;

- contact software and hardware vendors for product material and demonstrations.

Once candidates are identified and information from user and vendor sources is collected, use the 'must-have' requirements list to check the features that the component has and get scores for all candidates. If you find that you are comparing a large number of potential component combinations, use functional areas to identify a more manageable number of packages. You are unlikely to find a package that meets all the most important features so a scoring system will help identify the most suitable candidates for a shortlist of candidates. Ideally, two to four candidate packages will be identified for evaluation and testing. Table 10.3 shows an example of checking software packages by the most important features. This example uses a basic single-point scale for each feature, but a weighted scoring system may provide a more accurate picture.

Evaluate candidates – a checklist

Evaluating and testing software packages can be a difficult and time-consuming process. 'The challenge here will be evaluating the strengths and weaknesses of the various systems and selecting one that satisfies or most closely matches your goals' (Dilauro, 2004). Following an organised and structured process, and weeding out candidates before detailed evaluation, can help avoid an endless cycle of evaluation and experimentation.

A detailed checklist can provide some structure and organisation to the process. The checklist is completed and scored with information gathered from vendors, current users, publications and other sources. An important source of information is hands-on testing. This can be difficult and time-consuming, which is why you want to limit the number of candidate systems for in-depth evaluation. Open source software has some advantages, as it can be downloaded and installed in a test environment without payment to vendors. However, this is not completely free of cost as hardware and systems administration services must be available to set up the software. Some vendors will provide a trial version of their software, which can be installed and tested locally, as with open source software. However, make sure the trial version does not have any features disabled. Another alternative is to visit other institutions that will allow you to see and experiment with their installations.

Table 10.3 Comparing software packages by 'must-have' features

Feature	Software package					
	A	B	C	D	F	G
Content creation						
Content acquisition						
Bulk upload content files	✗	✓	✗	✗	✗	✗
Bulk upload metadata in XML	✓	✓	✓	✓	✓	✗
Export specified content files	✓	✗	✓	✓	✓	✗
Export specified metadata	✓	✓	✗	✗	✗	✗
File formats supported						
TIFF	✓	✓	✓	✓	✓	✓
JPEG	✓	✓	✓	✓	✓	✓
PDF	✓	✓	✓	✓	✓	✓
Metadata creation						
Support qualified Dublin Core descriptive metadata	✓	✓	✓	✓	✓	✓
Support XML-based hierarchical metadata schemas	✓	✗	✗	✗	✗	✗
Automatic link associated objects	✓	✓	✗	✗	✗	✓
Assemble multi-page objects	✓	✗	✗	✗	✗	✓
Content management						
Objects						
Add/delete objects	✓	✓	✗	✓	✓	✓
Auto generation of relationships	✓	✓	✗	✗	✗	✗
End-user interface						
Search						
Keywords	✓	✓	✓	✓	✓	✓
Full-text	✓	✓	✓	✓	✓	✓
Display						
Zooming and panning	✓	✓	✗	✗	✗	✗
Navigation						
Page turning	✓	✗	✓	✓	✗	✗
Operating systems						
Windows XP	✓	✓	✓	✓	✗	✗
More …						
Total	17	14	10	11	9	9

Even if you cannot test every system component under consideration, it is wise to test final candidate software packages completely before making a decision. This will help discover problems, bugs and issues that are not evident in the documentation. Representatives from all the groups who will use the software, including system administrators, metadata specialists, archivists, and so on, should participate in the testing. Pay particular attention to the features that satisfy the most critical organisational requirements that have been identified.

Goh and colleagues (2006) developed a checklist for evaluating open source digital library software. The checklist consists of 12 categories of items. Each category is divided into several subcategories of items. A group of four people trained in information science and familiar with digital library concepts assigned weights to each category and its respective items independently. The total sum of the category weights was 100, while the total sum of the items in each category was 10. Discrepancies were then resolved with face-to-face discussions in which each person provided justifications for their decisions. Pair-wise comparisons were also conducted as part of the process of formulating appropriate weights for the checklist.

The University of Arizona Library used a similar checklist and a weighted scoring system to evaluate software packages. They recommend that scoring be weighted according to organisational requirements (Han, 2004).

We adopted the concepts from both of these studies and combined them with our own experiences to create a checklist process using our 'FITS to O' model. This model first groups the requirements into four broad groups: functionality, interface, technology and support. Each group consists of several categories. Weights can be assigned to each category with an equal total (e.g. 100) in each group to reflect their equivalent importance. The categories are divided into subcategories, each of which contains items that can be checked. The total scores for each group are achieved by adding the weighted scores from each category. Each software package being evaluated is scored in the checklist and the total score for a package is the sum of the four groups. If you are evaluating different packages in different functional areas, then the checklists for each area may have different requirements, particularly in the functionality group.

The organisational considerations can contain characteristics of the original material, user requirements, budgets, compatibility, staff expertise, timeframe and strategic goals. Each category will be given a point from 1 to 5 (or 1 to 10) by the evaluation team. Points can also be allocated by adding up the points given by each reviewer and dividing by the number of reviewers to get the average score. Each category will be given a weight with a total of 100. The total score for each category is achieved by multiplying the point of each category by the weight of each category. The final score of a software package for organisational considerations is calculated by adding up all category scores.

The steps for applying the 'FITS to O' model to the checklist scoring process are:

1. Start with the checklist in Appendix A. You can add or remove items and categories according to your needs.

2. Assign a weight to each category with a total of 100 within each group (sample weights are assigned in Appendix A).

3. Assign a weight to each subcategory with a total of 10 within each category (sample weights are assigned in Appendix A).

4. Place a check mark for each item that exists in the software package being evaluated.

5. Within each subcategory,
   – multiply the number of check marks by the subcategory weight;
   – divide this resulting number by the number of items in the subcategory to obtain subcategory score.

6. Within each category, sum all subcategory scores, divide the total by 10, and multiply the resulting number by the category weight to obtain the category score.

7. Within each group, sum all category scores to obtain the group score.

8. Sum all group scores to obtain the total score for a software package.

9. Give between 1–5 points to a category in the 'organisational requirements and resources' table.

10. Assign a weight to each category in the 'organisational requirements and resources' table (sample weights are assigned in Appendix A).

11. Multiply the point by the weight in each category to obtain the total score for each category.

12. Sum all total scores to obtain the final score for the organisational considerations.

13. Sum the 'FITS' score and the 'O' score to obtain the final score for each software package.

The 'FITS to O' model provides a way to structure the software features to present a clear picture of the systems' relative ability to satisfy the selection criteria. Separate comparisons can be made for functionality, interface, technology and support. Organisational needs are the key in the process of selection. This model is very flexible; an evaluation team can make changes in the categories and subcategories, add or remove items, change wordings, and otherwise adapt to new information that is inevitably discovered as more is learned about the requirements and system offerings. This flexibility is necessary because there will always be surprises, no matter how well the selection process has been planned and organised.

Hardware selection

Our selection process has so far focused on software components. For the most part, hardware to support the DCMS will depend on the platform requirements of the selected software and the organisational requirements for compatibility. However, some hardware will need to be selected specifically for the DCMS, primarily to support digitisation. The process for selecting digitisation equipment is similar to the software selection process. The main differences are related to the different types of equipment available or required for digitising different types of material. For example, different kinds of scanners are used to create images from various types of original material:

- Flatbed scanners are suitable for scanning materials that can lay flat on a surface, such as papers, photographs and other printed materials.
- Film scanners are specially designed for scanning slides, 35-mm film and other transparent material. Dedicated film scanners usually produce better quality scans compared with flatbed scanners with transparency adapters.
- Book scanners or overhead scanners are designed to digitise books and other objects that cannot be laid flat.
- Large-format scanners were developed to digitise large-format materials such as maps and engineering drawings.
- Digital cameras can be used to digitise large-format materials, books and three-dimensional objects.

Another issue to consider is the software used to operate the scanner. Some digitisation and image manipulation software has the ability to acquire images directly from various kinds of scanners. In other systems, software that is packaged with the hardware is used to create image files that can be accessed by the image manipulation or digital object creation software.

The Western States Digital Standards Group (2003) has addressed several technical factors that will also influence digitisation equipment selection, including available optical resolution, bit depth, size of scan area, speed, connectivity and ability to handle different formats and materials in the collection. The document provides detailed information about how to select a scanner, and we refer readers there to learn the basic concepts. Digitisation technologies develop very quickly and new equipment emerges on the market every year, so we recommend that you consult independent reviews and vendor documentation for the most up-to-date and accurate information.

Other hardware required for a DCMS includes computer(s), high-resolution monitors, storage, and so on. Selection of such hardware has become relatively easy, and so will not be discussed here.

Case study: DCPC software selection for the DCMS

Organisational requirements

WRLC operates a distributed digital library system (known as ALADIN), which consists of a shared library automation system and online public-access catalogue (OPAC), a patron portal, and access to remote and local electronic resources. An important requirement identified when the DCPC was created and digitisation project begun was to make sure the digital collections were integrated with the ALADIN system. They should be discoverable and accessible within the same context as other local and remote electronic resources. Individual digital collections should be catalogued in the OPAC, accessible via the WRLC digital and special collections website, and linked from each member library's special collections webpage.

The WRLC member libraries host a variety of unique special collections that are being digitised in the DCPC. The types of material include manuscripts, photographs, slides, postcards, full-text documents, scrapbooks, newspaper clippings, audio recordings, and so forth. Because of the variety of material and content, the digital collections require different indexes and field display labels for the metadata. In addition, due to the consortium libraries' participation in various overlapping projects and systems, each digital collection needs to be independent. It is very important to make the libraries' digital collections available across multiple environments and accessible through multiple channels. The libraries may use individual digital objects outside the WRLC digital library system for online exhibits or other purposes. Digital files and their related metadata need to be independently accessible and in standard formats in order to be linked from other online systems.

Before the DCPC project started, the WRLC had created several digital collections for member libraries. These collections were created using OCLC's SiteSearch software. At the same time as the project started, the SiteSearch product was being dropped by OCLC and its future was uncertain. An important requirement for the new DCPC digital collections management system was thus the ability to migrate and import our existing collections.

Selection criteria

Selecting suitable software for the DCPC was a difficult task. We needed a system that could evolve as our requirements changed and we learned more about how the digital collections might be used. Standards are critical to that flexibility and we identified Dublin Core as the desired metadata format and XML as the desired encoding scheme. We also required that the software be extensible for adopting new standards and formats. The system had to be suitable to manage the features of multiple independent collections and to meet the requirements of our local workflow and procedures.

We were looking for two important user interfaces: a public user interface for presentation and a metadata creation interface for administration. For the public user interface, we needed a very good browsing feature as users may know nothing about a particular collection and browsing provides a good starting point to explore it. A powerful search engine was another important feature. The user interface should be easy to navigate and easy to customise. Each collection should be indexed and displayed separately. Individual digital objects and related metadata should be linkable from other webpages or systems. The system should have the ability to display multiple images and various document formats.

The data entry interface is crucial for staff to create metadata records efficiently. It is a tool to describe individual digital objects and their relationships. It is also used to retrieve and manage the master and derivative image files. It should allow staff to create templates, to view the digital object being described, to search, edit and delete records, to make global changes, and to have local authority control. An important feature is ease of use as staff at the member libraries will use this tool to edit and enhance their records but may not be specially trained in metadata creation.

Greenstone Digital Library Software

In 2002, when we were selecting our DCMS, the digital library software market was not mature and there were fewer offerings than there are today. We investigated and tested both commercial products and open source software and found no system that met our needs completely. We decided, therefore, to adapt two open source programs, DC-dot (*http://www.ukoln.ac.uk/metadata/dcdot*) for metadata creation and the Greenstone Digital Library Software (*http://www.greenstone.org*) for web delivery, in order to integrate them with each other and our existing digital library infrastructure. In general, we tried to avoid changing the original source code of these systems, relying instead on auxiliary scripts or plug-in modules to implement local functionality. These were written using open source and freely available tools, such as Perl (*http://www .perl-foundation.org*) for scripting and sgrep (*http://www.cs.helsinki.fi/u/ jjaakkol/sgrep.html*) for searching structured text files.

The Greenstone Digital Library Software, developed by the New Zealand Digital Library Project at the University of Waikato, had many features that met our requirements. These included a powerful search engine, metadata-based browsing facilities, and a customisable user interface. However, it lacked the tools required to create digital objects, such as a good metadata management interface based on the Dublin Core standard. We therefore customised Greenstone to import digital objects that we created with DC-dot. (The Greenstone team has since developed the 'Greenstone Librarian Interface', a graphical tool for creating and editing digital objects and collections.)

Selecting repository software

Greenstone also lacked support for the management and preservation of digital content, such as persistent object identifiers, migration tools, provenance information and authorisation levels. We therefore decided to manage our digital objects outside of Greenstone. The content files resided on a web server and were logically linked to the metadata by a file naming convention. The metadata files, along with URL links to the associated content files, were imported into Greenstone. The content files could only be updated via the server file system (not the web server), and made use of the server's authentication and authorisation to control access.

This lightweight repository implementation served the DCPC well for the first few years, while we had relatively few digital collections (a dozen or two), a modest number of digital objects (several thousand), and a limited number of administrators and managers centralised in one location. However, this implementation did not scale well as our collections grew and requirements changed. We identified the need for a more formal and structured repository to better automate and control management and preservation functions. Concurrent with that activity, in 2004, the consortium was evaluating DSpace, EPrints and ProQuest's Digital Commons service to support institutional repositories. We therefore decided to evaluate those systems in the context of digital collections management at the same time. We also experimented with the Fedora repository platform, which had recently had its first release as an open source project.

At the time, Fedora was a promising platform for building repository systems but the community, which has since contributed a rich set of Fedora workflow and dissemination tools, was just beginning to form. DSpace, which was selected as the consortium's institutional repository platform, was a more mature product with a complete submission workflow user interface and easy-to-use import tools for migrating our existing content. We chose DSpace to support our digital collections as the easiest and quickest way to implement the repository, while still maintaining the flexibility and transparency that comes with an open source system.

While the maturity of the DSpace product and community helped us set up the repository and import digital collections, we were less successful in adapting its workflow for submission of scholarly material to our processes for creating and describing digital objects. As described in the case study in Chapter 9, we created a web services interface to integrate DSpace with our digital object creation and dissemination tools. The selection of an open repository system has eased the integration with other components of the DCMS, which we continue to enhance.

11

Documentation

The importance of documentation

Good documentation is the recording of key decisions and procedures of a digitisation project, and is essential for successfully completing current and future projects. There are many benefits of creating good project documentation. It helps speed up the progress of the project by avoiding repetition or conflicting solutions. It also helps reduce mistakes and saves time in the execution of technical procedures. Documentation can improve communications and support rapid decision-making throughout the project. It is invaluable to keeping a digitisation project progressing in the right direction if there are unplanned changes in project staff or management. Good documentation can also facilitate the long-term maintenance and enhancement of the digital collection, as well as enable future systems and data migrations. The continuity provided by documentation will be of benefit throughout the lifetime of the digital collection.

How to document a project and what to document

Major issues and elements that may be included in documentation are:

- project goals and mission;
- decisions made for major issues;
- rationales for each decision;
- rationales for selecting software and hardware, as well as standards regarding metadata and digitisation;

- responsibilities of each party involved;
- time schedule;
- major workflow;
- technical details.

Project information may be documented in a variety of formal and informal formats. Official or formal documents, such as grant applications, project reports, guidelines, and so on, may be published, and become guides for other institutions that are planning for digitisation projects. Other documents, such as project or workflow plans, procedures, schedules, system user manuals, project statistics, meeting minutes, e-mail messages, and so on, should be kept internally for future reference.

There are many ways to document a digitisation project. The project manager or management team should report the progress of the project periodically, documenting problems and solutions at each stage and the decisions made for major issues. The staff or project team responsible for each aspect of the project should keep appropriate documentation recording the rationale for each action, system user manuals, various instructions for scanning, image creation and conversion, metadata creation, data mapping, and so on. Technology has made it easier to keep good records of even informal communications. Blogs, discussion forums, e-mail lists, project management software, problem reporting databases, and so forth, are good tools for documenting project communications. A project website, organisational intranet, and project directory on a local file server are some examples of tools and mechanisms that can be used to deliver and save project documentation.

The major kinds of digitisation project documents include planning documents, management documents and technical documents.

Planning documents

Planning documents record major issues, decisions, plans and actions during the planning process. As Wisser (2005) points out, 'documentation strategies are an essential aspect of the planning process, as details and decisions made during the planning process can guide the project'.

One lesson we learned from our own experience is that it is very important to start documenting as soon as the planning process begins. Some material selected from one participating institution was questioned during the planning process of a large collaborative digitisation project. Representatives from other participating institutions argued that those materials should not be selected for the collection, while the representative from the institution that did the selection insisted the materials were appropriate according to the selection criteria. Unfortunately, nobody could find the selection criteria documented anywhere. No written documentation, meeting minutes, even e-mail exchanges, recording the selection decisions were available for verifying this matter. The project was delayed by the interruption and the relationship between the partners was strained by this episode. Good documentation would have prevented the delay and the bad feelings.

Examples of planning documents include:

- grant application or request for funding;
- project budget;
- job descriptions for project staff;
- committee membership and charges;
- decisions made on selecting equipment, software and metadata standards, as well as the rationales for the decisions;
- request for information (RFI) or request for proposal (RFP) if any work is contracted;
- material selection criteria;
- minutes from planning meetings;
- project proposal;
- project timeline.

Management documents

Management documents record the tasks, decisions, processes, procedures, schedules, workflow, work statistics, and so on, that take place during the project. A digitisation project manager must know how to document the management process, which will help him or her perform the project management duties intelligently and efficiently. Proper management documentation is especially important for digital conversion services where various digitisation projects are going on simultaneously and each individual project requires special attention and different treatments.

It will take time to document a process, to summarise what has been decided and what has been implemented. It will also take time for people involved in the project to read the documentation. In addition, writing project documentation is often not as professionally interesting and satisfying as designing, building, testing and delivering digital collections, and some staff may not think it is necessary to spend time documenting and reviewing documentation. However, from our own experience we have learned that it is very important not to cut corners when it comes to management documentation as it is essential for working efficiently and avoiding mistakes during a project and in future projects.

Examples of management documents include:

- the project plan;
- project status reports that document and summarise progress, issues and problems during a particular stage or period of time;
- copyright clearance documentation;
- workflow and schedule plans;
- material receiving and returning procedures and records;
- guidelines for handling materials;
- production statistics;
- meeting minutes;
- e-mail discussions;
- completed project summary report.

Technical documents

Technical documents include a variety of technical information. As technology changes so rapidly, it is very important to document in detail the decisions made in using certain technology, such as when and why the decision was made, who made the decision, what solution was used to fix a technical problem, what ideas did not work, and so on. Documenting technical processes, procedures and best practices is a task that takes extra time and may be considered boring and mundane. However, without meaningful documentation, the project staff may spend more time dealing with technical problems, repeatedly researching and collecting information, and implementing different flavours of the same technical solutions. All this results in more work and wasted time.

One of the worst nightmares for technology-related projects is when a member of the technical staff leaves the project and the project stalls because the staff member did not provide sufficient documentation for another staff member to figure out how the systems and processes are implemented. One library in our consortium has a home-grown archival collection data system that was developed by a staff member who worked on this system for over 20 years. The staff member passed away several years ago and the library has not been able to successfully retrieve all the data due to a lack of documentation on how to use the system.

Keeping too much technical information can be overwhelming. It is important to know what should be documented and what need not be kept. This knowledge only comes from experience. Before that experience is gained, staff should err on the side of keeping too much documentation, including as much detailed technical information as possible, to establish a habit for documentation. After several projects, one can see what documentation has been used regularly or provided critical information. It is also important to organise the technical documentation in a way that can be recalled and retrieved easily. If you do not remember where you stored the technical documentation and cannot locate it, all the time you spent on documenting the process is wasted.

Examples of technical documents include:

- scanning specifications;
- instructions or manuals for using system software, equipment, and so on;
- instructions for creating metadata and mapping metadata elements;
- technical metadata embedded in the images;
- detailed workflow descriptions;
- 'how to' documents describing how to perform various tasks;
- changes made when upgrading to a new version of a software application;
- problem reports and solutions;
- technical feature requests;
- e-mails discussing technical problems;
- notes and explanations in system configuration files;
- comments in scripts describing the automation steps.

Statistics

Collecting appropriate statistics is an important part of the documentation process and is essential for managing and tracking the progress of digitisation projects and programmes.

There are two types of statistics: production statistics and usage statistics.

Production statistics provide information about how much work has been done by whom. These statistics help management track the cost and staff time expended on each project and to determine future project plans. 'Used properly, they can highlight service gaps and opportunities and help us determine what to allocate for budgets' (Singh, 2005).

Examples of project production statistics include:

- pages scanned daily, monthly and yearly;
- pages scanned for each project;
- metadata created daily, monthly and yearly;
- metadata created for each project;
- number of derivative files created for each project;
- number of web pages created for each project;
- number of projects completed each year.

Usage statistics provide information about how often the collections and the images are used; who is using the collections; where users are based; which search engines or indexing agents refer users to the collections; which collections, objects and image files are used most; how users search the collections and discover interesting material; what kinds of computers are used to access the images, and so forth. Usage statistics are very important factors for evaluating the success and value of a project. Analysing usage statistics will help improve access by informing more accessible web presentations, determining appropriate distribution and dissemination channels, making adjustments in future projects, and so on.

Statistics should be collected automatically whenever possible. For example, web servers typically log all requests and various tools are available for producing usage reports from those logs.

Case study: DCPC's documentation

The DCPC is a centralised digital conversion facility that typically has several projects running concurrently. Documenting each project appropriately is very important for making effective plans and tracking the progress of each project. Types of documentation are given below.

Project plan

The project plan contains the name of the owning library, a general description of the physical collection, the title of the digital collection, the collection scope, any use restrictions, delivery and retrieval plans for the original materials, any special handling requirements, target timelines, and owning library contact information (see Appendix B, sample 1).

Copyright status

We require the owning library to affirm that it has the right to digitise the material in the collection. We keep a signed copyright status form (see Appendix B, sample 2). In cases where works to be digitised are covered by copyright, the owning library is responsible for obtaining permission to digitise and disseminate the works from the copyright holder. A copy of the permissions document must be provided to the DCPC, along with the materials to digitise.

Material characteristics and scanning specifications

After receiving the materials, we review and analyse the original items, identify and document significant characteristics of the material, and specify scanning parameters according to our established standard. See Appendix B, sample 3 for an example of this simple documentation.

Sample metadata records

Since we selected qualified Dublin Core as the DCPC's descriptive metadata standard, we do not need to choose a metadata standard for each collection. However, as each collection is different and information accompanying the original material varies, we need to select appropriate Dublin Core elements for each collection and, when the owning library provides some information about each item, we need to determine how to map the information to appropriate Dublin Core fields. This mapping often includes simple transformations to put the metadata in the appropriate format, such as translating textual data fields to a standard numeric form. We also need to design structural metadata according to the characteristics of the originals. For each project, we create some sample records along with suggestions in broad subject headings and keywords and send to the owning library for review and approval. This document will guide us in creating metadata records (see Appendix B, sample 4).

Project summary

After a project is completed, we provide a project summary to the owning library. The project summary includes the number of pages scanned, number of records created, date the project is finished, and the date it is launched on the web. As we have created a MARC record for each collection in our library catalogue, we include the record number in the project summary (see Appendix B, sample 5).

Production statistics

We keep daily, monthly and yearly production statistics categorised by project and institution. These statistics have helped the management in decision making, project planning, scheduling, storage managing, quality control and productivity managing.

Use statistics

The usage statistics for the digital collections are collected and presented to the library staff through the WRLC libraries intranet. The usage statistics provide helpful information on how often a collection is visited, how many times a digital object is requested, where the users come from, and what browser they are using. These statistics assist the library staff in determining how to select other collections for digitisation, and they help DCPC management make decisions regarding interface design and software selection.

Technical documents

We document major technical decisions made in each individual digitisation project, including file naming convention, metadata design, user interface functionality requirements, metadata mapping and transformations, metadata input instructions, technical issues and problems resolved, and so on. For non-routine tasks and special processes, we write down step-by-step instructions. This helps save time later should we encounter a similar situation in another project.

Many technical details differ from project to project and there are many ways to document these details. We try our best to record the changes in configuration files and to make special notes regarding any technical changes. We also document scanning techniques and the Photoshop conversion process for different types of materials.

Procedural documents

As we deal mostly with materials from archives and special collections, we make every effort to keep these precious materials secure. When we return the material to the owning library, we require a signature from the person who receives the material. The signed return slip is kept for documentation. We also scan the return slip and convert it to electronic form so that we can access it from any computer when we do not have access to the paper slip.

12

The knowledge and skills required for creating digital collections

Creating digital collections is an extremely complex task. Any digitisation project, whether it is a grant-funded digitisation project or a library-sponsored project, a single institution's digitisation project or a multi-institutional collaborative project, a task-oriented project or an ongoing digital collections programme, requires people with a variety of skills and knowledge.

Digitisation project staff may include any combination of the following: advisory committee, project manager, curatorial staff, archive staff, subject specialist, metadata specialist or cataloguer, scanning technician, systems administrator, programmer, graphic designer and web designer. Digitisation projects almost always demand a team effort. Institutions vary in their areas of expertise. Smaller institutions may have a team with few members, each working on a mix of tasks. Large institutions and large projects may be able to hire area specialists concentrating on a specific aspect of the project.

As Tanner (2001) points out, people with the requisite mix of project experience and technical ability are in short supply for staffing digitisation projects at present and it will take time before enough projects have been completed to deliver experienced people into the wider workforce. Several years have passed since Tanner's writing, yet as more digitisation projects have been completed and more training opportunities are available, people with the required knowledge and skills in digitisation are still in demand. This is because as internet technology develops, stakeholders' expectations for digitisation projects rise, thus requiring staff with updated and expanded knowledge and skills to produce high-quality digital collections with powerful functionality and usability.

Choi and Rasmussen surveyed 'digital librarians' in 39 academic and research libraries in the USA:

> Participants were asked to rate the importance of skills and knowledge in performing their work for three areas – technical areas, traditional library-related areas, and other skills – with 23 sub-areas on a 5-point Likert scale. The five highest ranked choices among all sub-areas were communication and interpersonal skills (mean 4.60), project management/leadership skills (4.56), understanding of digital library architecture and software (4.52), knowledge of the needs of users (4.42), and knowledge of technical and quality standards (4.33). (Choi and Rasmussen, 2006)

Because of the complexity of digitisation projects, digitisation professionals are clearly required to have more breadth and depth of knowledge and skills in management, technology and human relations. It is difficult to itemise all the desirable knowledge and skills for staffing digitisation projects as different projects require different skills. However, we will list key qualities in the major areas. This list does not comprise job descriptions for different jobs, rather it enumerates knowledge and skills needed to accomplish the task. For example, many digitisation projects hire student workers and interns to scan materials. The student workers and interns may not need to have all the knowledge and skills listed under 'Scanning'. They will, however, need clear instructions for the scanning work and the ability to follow those instructions. The list includes the knowledge and skills required to provide instructions for the student workers to finish the scanning work.

Management

Good management is vital for a successful digitisation project because of the unpredictable changes in the technology, the complex nature of the digitisation process, and the high-level skills and training required from project staff. A manager or a management team does not need hands-on experience of all aspects of a digitisation project but must understand the process and be able to lead the project in the correct direction while keeping it within the time and cost constraints. The following knowledge and skills are the key qualities for managing digitisation projects:

- strong leadership capability and clear understanding of goals of and issues related to creating digital collections;

- effective communication and interpersonal skills for working with project staff that may be diverse in expertise, location and temperament;
- overall understanding of the digital collections infrastructure, including processes, standards and technology;
- knowledge of current digitisation technologies, standards and best practices;
- knowledge of policies, procedures and intellectual property rights involved in digitisation;
- knowledge of requirements analysis, project planning and tracking, task prioritisation and workflow management;
- understanding of the costs involved in digitisation and knowledge of funding opportunities available for projects;
- understanding of the importance of project documentation and statistics reporting;
- marketing skills to disseminate, promote and publicise digital collections.

Material selection

The task of selecting material for digitisation is often fulfilled by staff in library archives and special collections and by subject specialists. Selection for digitisation is a complicated process that requires professionals with specific knowledge and skills:

- knowledge of content and subjects of the collection which can provide sound justifications for selection decisions;
- knowledge of collection development issues and understanding of how collection development relates to organisational mission and goals;
- in-depth understanding of intellectual property rights and how to research and obtain copyright permission;
- understanding of the purpose of digitisation and current digitisation technologies and best practices;
- ability to develop selection criteria and to document selecting decisions;
- understanding of user and institutional requirements;
- understanding of traditional and digital preservation issues;
- knowledge of digital file formats and methods of conversion;
- understanding of the importance of metadata and preparing material for digitisation.

Scanning

Scanning requires a unique set of skills and knowledge. Any scanning project, whether it is done in-house by experienced scanning technicians or student workers, or outsourced to commercial scanning vendors, requires knowledge of scanning hardware and software. Scanning is time-consuming and expensive, so in-depth knowledge and skills in the following areas are essential for planning and instructing a scanning project, regardless of who is actually performing the work:

- knowledge of scanning technologies and terminologies;
- understanding of image file formats and methods of conversion between formats;
- experience using a variety of digitisation devices, including flatbed scanners, film scanners and digital cameras;
- experience using scanner software and image processing applications;
- understanding of the concepts and roles of master and derivative files;
- experience in image processing, such as cropping, retouching, scaling, resizing, editing, and so on;
- knowledge of batch image processing and ability to set up batch jobs;
- understanding of the role and implementation of file naming conventions;
- understanding of administrative and structural metadata;
- knowledge of benchmarking, quality control and assessment of scanning products;
- understanding of the characteristics of archival material and material handling guidelines;
- attention to detail;
- ability to manage workflow and record statistics and documentation.

Metadata

This area involves metadata design and metadata creation. Designing metadata, especially structural metadata, requires in-depth knowledge of metadata standards, schemas, tools, technology and user interface design. Non-professionals such as technicians, student workers or interns can enter simple metadata if subject headings or controlled vocabularies are given. Professional metadata specialists with the ability to perform subject analysis and assign subject headings are required for more extensive metadata creation. Metadata can also be created automatically by programming or converting from other databases and applications. Despite how metadata are created, to fulfil the task, the following knowledge and skills are required:

- knowledge of metadata standards, schemas, best practices and applications;
- knowledge of controlled vocabularies and authority control;
- understanding of crosswalks between metadata schemas;
- ability to design structural metadata and administrative metadata;
- understanding of a variety of digital file formats;
- ability to select and apply appropriate standards and good practices based on the type of material and the objectives of a particular digital project;
- ability to design a metadata structure for automatic metadata creation;
- experience using a variety of metadata creation tools;
- understanding of the importance of consistency in metadata creation, and attention to detail;
- ability to be flexible and efficient;
- understanding of user search and discovery behaviour;
- working knowledge of XML;
- experience using different databases and applications, and understanding of data migration and conversion between databases and applications;
- knowledge of user interface design and its relationship to metadata design and creation.

User interface

User interface design for digital collections is often a collaboration between public service librarians, subject specialists, graphic designers, web designers, system administrators and end users. Graphic and web design may be done in-house or outsourced to commercial graphic designers or a web design firm. When the design is completed, the user interface can be configured and implemented by in-house staff. The following knowledge and skills are required to accomplish the task:

- knowledge of the digital collections presentation system being used, including ability to configure the system;
- knowledge of current technologies, standards, rules, encoding languages and applications for web design;
- understanding of user and institutional requirements;
- understanding of the topics and content of the digital collection;
- knowledge of graphic design theory and application;
- experience with software applications to create web graphics;
- understanding of metadata elements, especially the structural metadata elements used for navigation in the collection.

Information technology

Information technology support is required for any kind of digitisation project. Larger libraries and collaborative efforts may have IT staff dedicated to digital collections projects. Most small to medium-sized libraries, however, depend on institutional IT resources to provide computer and network services such as systems administration and hardware maintenance. In any case, it is important for digital collections staff to be knowledgeable and able to communicate effectively about technology. This requires skills beyond computer *literacy* or the ability to use computers. Computer *fluency*, which adds problem solving and complexity management skills, is required for effective communication of technical requirements and issues. In addition, as noted by Dahl and colleagues (2006), 'a number of inexpensive and widely adopted "enabling technologies" ... allow local libraries to seize control of their digital library environment'. As digital collections staff move from understanding to working knowledge in these areas they will be able to implement and enhance their infrastructure with less dependence on the organisation's IT department:

- knowledge of web servers and transport protocol (e.g. HTTP);
- knowledge of web and batch scripting languages such as Perl, PHP, Cold Fusion and Microsoft's Active Server Pages;

- knowledge of XML technologies such as XSLT, XPath, and DOM and SAX parsers;
- understanding of XML-based schemas for encoding metadata standards;
- knowledge of the server operating system used for digital collections management and presentation, such as Microsoft Windows Server, Linux or Unix;
- ability to download, install and configure open source software on the server operating system;
- knowledge of relational databases and other tools for storing, indexing and searching information;
- understanding of the importance of data backup and ability to specify a backup strategy to protect against data loss.

Key qualities

In addition to the knowledge and skills required for each area of digitisation, a set of key qualities for working in the digitisation field is critical:

- flexibility;
- capacity to learn constantly and quickly;
- willingness to adopt changes and learn new skills;
- effective communication and interpersonal skills;
- team work;
- capacity and desire to work independently;
- risk-taking;
- organisational skills;
- documentation skills.

13

Conclusion

At the beginning of this book, we described the benefits of and demands for creating and preserving digital collections. The factors that are motivating digitisation are increasing rapidly, and the pressure to expose the information and knowledge in special collections and archives on the web will continue to grow. However, budget constraints within cultural institutions mean that the resources for digitisation are not likely to increase at the same rate. To meet the accelerating demand, digitisation, management and preservation need to be done in much more economical ways than they have in the past.

Mass digitisation efforts, such as Google Book Search (*http://books.google.com/googlebooks/about.html*) and the Open Content Alliance (*http://www.opencontentalliance.org*), are contributing to the expectation that digitisation can be done quickly, affordably and comprehensively. These projects use streamlined processes and advanced technology to scan books in bulk for about 10 cents a page (Albanese, 2007). Can this be done for special collections? Probably not, as the kinds of material in special collections vary more than manuscripts and therefore require more special handling. However, adopting the philosophy of mass digitisation can help bring down the costs of digital collection creation and management significantly and enable far greater rates of digitisation.

The librarians, archivists and curators who maintain our special collections are professionals with a long tradition of careful acquisition, description and management of primary source material. This has historically been very important for the preservation of unique and fragile physical materials. However, the requirements for digital material may be different, especially if you accept the mass-digitisation philosophy that it is more important to progress towards complete digitisation than to select a few resources to digitise and publish online in the highest quality. As Erway and Schaffner note (2007), 'scaling up digitization of special collections ... will compel us to temper our historical emphasis on quality with the recognition that large quantities of digitized special collections materials will better serve our users'.

With this recognition, organisations can embrace more economical and streamlined processes for digitisation. The requirements for these optimised digital collections creation and management processes can be summed up with three actions: integrate, automate and collaborate.

- *Integrate*: Rather than focusing on external fund-supported and project-based digitisation, these activities need to be integrated into routine day-to-day operations in order to accelerate the rate of digitisation and to protect the millions of dollars of investment in digitisation made to date. According to a survey conducted by the Northeast Document Conservation Center in 2005, 92 per cent of the institutions responding were creating digital materials yet only 29 per cent of these reported having written policies to address the management or preservation of digital assets. A high number of institutions reported having no or low levels of institutional funds allocated for the creation, acquisition, management or sustainability of digital collections (Clareson, 2006). Smith (2003) points out that the hardest part of sustainability is 'how to pay for it all'. The typical model of funding special projects to digitise collections will never support large-scale digitisation. Rather, the digitisation needs to be integrated with the routine accessioning and processing workflows in special collections and archives. Similarly, digitisation should be integrated with the process of fulfilling access requests for special collections material. In addition, the description and access to the digitised content can be integrated with the existing processes to describe collections with finding aids and item lists. The creation and management of digital collections is thus institutionalised as an integral part of the everyday operations of the organisation.

- *Automate*: Throughout the book we have stressed the importance of automating as much of the digital content, metadata creation and ongoing maintenance as possible. Here we explicitly state what this implies: compromises on image quality or metadata detail may be acceptable or even desirable in order to automate and streamline the digital collections processes. As described earlier, automated OCR can compensate for a lack of specific high-quality descriptive metadata. In addition, once users of the online material have access to it, metadata quality can be improved through tagging and web annotation systems. Quality can be revisited for those materials in greatest demand. But you can never be sure which collections deserve that extra attention and expense until you provide some base level of online access for them through automated processes such as high-speed scanning and metadata generation.

- *Collaborate*: Even with high degrees of integration and automation, only the largest institutions will be able to approach mass-digitisation rates. For the rest of us, we must to collaborate with others to share costs and expertise. The DCPC described in the case studies throughout this book is an example of a centralised digitisation centre with significant advantages in digital collections development and maintenance. A central facility can provide and retain the technical and managerial expertise that individual institutions cannot afford. Moreover, a shared facility can help ensure the long-term sustainability and institutionalisation of digital collections management. The DCPC's experiences present a model for sustaining digital collections in a centralised digital collection facility. Through concentrated technical expertise, combined financial resources, consolidated project management, and shared digital library systems the individual member libraries can create and sustain their digital collections at lower and affordable prices. For institutions without access to or resources for a centralised shared digital collections production centre, collaboration can occur on a more informal basis with similar institutions, it can occur between the library or archive departments and academic and technology departments within the institution, and it can involve outsourcing digitisation to a capable commercial firm. The same mass-digitisation projects that are transforming the expectations that users and institutions have about digitisation may also provide opportunities for collaboration as they start looking beyond manuscripts at the unique holdings and source material in special collections and archives.

Increasingly, special collections contain the knowledge and information that distinguish our cultural institutions. The processes, techniques and practices described in this book lay a foundation for bringing these materials online and making them accessible to much wider audiences. By integrating these practices with everyday operations, automating processes to provide more throughput and efficiency, and collaborating with partners to share the costs and expertise, greater quantities of material in the special collections of libraries, archives and museums will be exposed to the mainstream of the online world.

Appendix A:
Checklist for evaluating a digital collections management system

1. Add or remove items and categories according to your needs.
2. Assign a weight to each category with a total of 100 within each group (sample weights are assigned).
3. Assign a weight to each subcategory with a total of 10 within each category (sample weights are assigned).
4. Place a check mark for each item that exists in the software package being evaluated.
5. Within each subcategory,
   - Multiply the number of check marks by the subcategory weight.
   - Divide this resulting number by the number of items in the subcategory to obtain subcategory score.
6. Within each category, sum all subcategory scores, divide the total by 10, and multiply the resulting number by the category weight to obtain the category score.
7. Within each group, sum all category scores to obtain group score.
8. Sum all group scores to obtain the total score for a software package.

Functionality

Categories			Weight	
1 Content creation				**25%**
1.1 Content acquisition			**3.00**	
1.1.1 Batch upload content files	☐			
1.1.2 Upload from specified place (disk/folder/URL)	☐			
1.1.3 Acquire content files from scanner	☐			
1.1.4 Batch upload metadata	☐			
1.1.5 Import from spreadsheets and databases	☐			
1.1.6 Import collections from other systems	☐			
1.1.7 Import metadata in XML	☐			
Subcategory score (# of checks × weight)/# of items = (# of checks × 3)/6				
1.2 File formats supported			**2.00**	
1.2.1 TIFF	☐			
1.2.2 JPEG	☐			
1.2.3 GIF	☐			
1.2.4 JPEG 2000	☐			
1.2.5 PDF	☐			
1.2.6 Other	☐			
Subcategory score (# of checks × 2)/6				
1.3 File conversion			**1.00**	
1.3.1 Auto create display files	☐			
1.3.2 Auto create thumbnails	☐			
1.3.3 OCR capability and PDF creation	☐			
Subcategory score (# of checks × 1)/3				
1.4 Metadata creation			**4.00**	
1.4.1 Metadata schemas supported				
1.4.1.1 Dublin Core (qualified and unqualified)	☐			
1.4.1.2 DIDL	☐			
1.4.1.3 METS	☐			

Categories			Weight	
	1.4.1.4 MODS	☐		
	1.4.1.5 MARC	☐		
	1.4.1.6 Other	☐		
1.4.2	Define new metadata sets	☐		
1.4.3	Extract technical metadata from content files	☐		
1.4.4	Controlled vocabulary	☐		
1.4.5	Automatic link associated objects	☐		
1.4.6	Assemble multi-page objects	☐		
1.4.7	Crosswalk			
	1.4.7.1 MARC to Dublin Core	☐		
	1.4.7.2 Dublin Core to MARC	☐		
	1.4.7.3 Dublin Core to METS	☐		
	1.4.7.4 Other	☐		
1.4.8	Unicode character support	☐		
Subcategory score (# of checks × 4)/16				
Category: Content creation total score (Total of subcategory/10) × 25%				
2 Content management				25%
2.1 Collections			3.00	
2.1.1	Allow separate collections	☐		
2.1.2	Allow different interface for each collection	☐		
Subcategory score				
2.2 Objects			2.00	
2.2.1	Add/delete objects	☐		
2.2.2	Global delete content files/metadata records	☐		
2.2.3	Global update metadata records	☐		
2.2.4	Support for relationships between objects	☐		
2.2.5	Auto generation of relationships	☐		
2.2.6	Provenance documentation	☐		
Subcategory score				

Categories		Weight	
2.3 **Collection building**		**2.00**	
2.3.1 Auto build collection if a change is detected	☐		
2.3.2 Scheduled auto building of collections	☐		
Subcategory score			
2.4 **Access control**		**2.00**	
2.4.1 Limit access at different levels			
2.4.1.1 Object level	☐		
2.4.1.2 Collection level	☐		
2.4.1.3 Controlled access to master file	☐		
2.4.2 User selected password	☐		
2.4.3 Forgotten password retrieval	☐		
2.4.4 Limit access by group	☐		
2.4.5 Limit access by role	☐		
2.4.6 Create/remove user profile	☐		
2.4.7 Rights management	☐		
Subcategory score			
2.5 **Statistics and reports**		**1.00**	
2.5.1 Daily/monthly statistics of objects uploaded	☐		
2.5.2 Daily/monthly statistics of metadata created	☐		
2.5.3 Use report	☐		
Subcategory score			
Category: Content management total score			
3 **Content discovery**			**20%**
3.1 **Query features**		**4.00**	
3.1.1 Search specific collection	☐		
3.1.2 Search selected or all collections	☐		
3.1.3 Boolean logic	☐		
3.1.4 Proximity	☐		
3.1.5 Case insensitive search	☐		
3.1.6 Truncation or wild cards	☐		
3.1.7 Word stemming	☐		
3.1.8 Search selected metadata fields	☐		
Subcategory score			

Categories		Weight	
3.2 Browse features		**3.00**	
3.2.1 Set browse options by any metadata	☐		
3.2.2 Hierarchical browse	☐		
3.2.3 Sort browse lists by choice	☐		
3.2.4 Browse new submissions	☐		
Subcategory score			
3.3 Interoperability		**3.00**	
3.3.1 OAI-PMH	☐		
3.3.2 Z39.50	☐		
3.3.3 SRU/W	☐		
3.3.4 OpenURL	☐		
Subcategory score			
Category: Content discovery total score			
4 Content presentation			**15%**
4.1 Delivery mechanism		**5.00**	
4.1.1 Web	☐		
4.1.2 Intranet	☐		
4.1.3 CD-ROM/DVD	☐		
4.1.4 Portable devices	☐		
Subcategory score			
4.2 Supported browsers		**5.00**	
4.2.1 Internet Explorer v5.0 or later	☐		
4.2.2 Netscape v4.0 or later	☐		
4.2.3 Mozilla Firefox	☐		
Subcategory score			
Category: Content presentation total score			
5 Content preservation			**15%**
5.1 Object identification		**5.00**	
5.1.1 Persistent identifier for objects	☐		
5.1.2 Persistent URL for each collection	☐		
Subcategory score			
5.2 Version control		**2.50**	
5.2.1 Compare changes	☐		
5.2.2 Identify changes	☐		
5.2.3 Identify who made changes	☐		

Categories		Weight		
5.2.4 Allow different versions of content files/metadata records				
Subcategory score				
5.3 Content file control		**2.50**		
5.3.1 Auto identify content file formats	☐			
5.3.2 Content file format registry	☐			
5.3.3 Support multiple redundant copies	☐			
5.3.4 Migrate to different storage	☐			
Subcategory score				
Category: Content preservation total score				
Functionality total score				

Interface

Categories		Weight		
1 Staff interface				40%
1.1 Authoring		**1.00**		
1.1.1 Web interface	☐			
1.1.2 Allow remote access	☐			
1.1.3 Allow different levels of authoring	☐			
1.1.4 Multiple users use simultaneously	☐			
Subcategory score				
1.2 Metadata creation		**2.00**		
1.2.1 Templates setup	☐			
1.2.2 Define and change width of metadata fields	☐			
1.2.3 Add/remove metadata elements	☐			
1.2.4 View images and metadata template side by side	☐			
1.2.5 Tool for inputting special characters	☐			
1.2.6 Spelling check	☐			
1.2.7 Auto insert dynamic values (date of creation, etc.)	☐			
1.2.8 Pickup list of controlled vocabularies	☐			
Subcategory score				

Categories		Weight	
1.3 Search/browse		**1.50**	
1.3.1 By any metadata elements	☐		
1.3.2 By filename/identifier	☐		
1.3.3 By date of creation	☐		
1.3.4 By metadata creator	☐		
Subcategory score			
1.4 Customisation		**1.00**	
1.4.1 Can customise staff user interface	☐		
1.4.2 Work-in-process records	☐		
1.4.3 My records	☐		
Subcategory score			
1.5 Configuration of end-user interface		**2.00**	
1.5.1 Define/select search and browse options	☐		
1.5.2 Define/select plug-ins	☐		
1.5.3 Define/select indexes	☐		
1.5.4 HTML templates	☐		
1.5.5 Change colours and fonts	☐		
1.5.6 JavaScript generation	☐		
1.5.7 Graphic editing	☐		
Subcategory score			
1.6 Administrative tools		**1.50**	
1.6.1 Import/export objects	☐		
1.6.2 Import/export metadata	☐		
1.6.3 Create community/collection	☐		
1.6.4 Build collection	☐		
1.6.5 Assign rights and permissions	☐		
1.6.6 Create user profile	☐		
Subcategory score			
1.7 Help		**1.00**	
1.7.1 Explanation of each tool	☐		
1.7.2 Tutorial	☐		
1.7.3 Examples	☐		
Subcategory score			
Category: Staff interface total score			

Categories		Weight	
2 End-user interface			**60%**
2.1 Search		**3.00**	
2.1.1 Keywords	☐		
2.1.2 Full-text	☐		
2.1.3 Boolean	☐		
2.1.4 By any metadata elements	☐		
2.1.5 Proximity	☐		
2.1.6 Cross-collection	☐		
2.1.7 Display search results in thumbnails/text	☐		
Subcategory score			
2.2 Browse		**3.00**	
2.2.1 By any metadata elements	☐		
2.2.2 By thumbnails	☐		
Subcategory score			
2.3 Viewing/navigation		**1.50**	
2.3.1 Page turning	☐		
2.3.2 Zooming and panning	☐		
2.3.3 Flash files	☐		
2.3.4 JPEG 2000 files	☐		
2.3.5 Multiple views	☐		
2.3.6 Consistent header and footer	☐		
2.3.7 Link back to collection	☐		
2.3.8 Easy to set up preferences	☐		
Subcategory score			
2.4 Personalised		**1.00**	
2.4.1 My favourites	☐		
2.4.2 Create custom slide shows	☐		
2.4.3 RSS	☐		
Subcategory score			
2.5 Support		**1.50**	
2.5.1 Questions/comments	☐		
2.5.2 Report problems	☐		
2.5.3 Guides/help	☐		
Subcategory score			
Category: End-user interface total score			
Interface total score			

Technology

Categories		Weight	
1 Openness			**25%**
1.1 Open source		**3.00**	
1.1.1 View, modify and distribute source code	☐		
Subcategory score			
1.2 Open services		**3.00**	
1.2.1 Web service to access system functionality	☐		
1.2.2 Other API to access system functionality	☐		
1.2.3 Adding functionality through third-party plug-ins	☐		
Subcategory score			
1.3 Open data		**4.00**	
1.3.1 Standard query language	☐		
1.3.2 Export/harvest digital objects	☐		
1.3.3 Batch import digital objects			
Subcategory score			
Category: Openness total score			
2 Scalability			**20%**
2.1 Number of content files		**1.00**	
2.1.1 30,000+	☐		
2.1.2 50,000+	☐		
2.1.3 No limit	☐		
Subcategory score			
2.2 Number of metadata records		**1.00**	
2.2.1 30,000+	☐		
2.2.2 50,000+	☐		
2.2.3 No limit	☐		
Subcategory score			
2.3 Performance of large collections		**3.00**	
2.3.1 Fast searching	☐		
2.3.2 Fast indexing	☐		
2.3.3 No difference when more users used simultaneously	☐		
Subcategory score			

Categories				Weight	
2.4	**Hardware performance**			**3.00**	
	2.4.1	Performance scales with hardware upgrades	☐		
	2.4.2	Allow distributing programs over multiple servers	☐		
	Subcategory score				
Category: Scalability total score					
3	**Reliability**				**20%**
3.1	No reported components failure		☐	2.00	
3.2	Accurate results of service request		☐	2.00	
3.3	Reported uptime >99%		☐	2.00	
3.4	No reported corrupted content files		☐	2.00	
3.5	No reported corrupted metadata records		☐	2.00	
Category: Reliability total score					
4	**Flexibility**				**20%**
4.1	**Architecture**			**2.00**	
	4.1.1	Open architecture	☐		
	4.1.2	Support multiple file formats	☐		
	Subcategory score				
4.2	**Tools for configuration**			**3.00**	
	4.2.1	Stylesheet	☐		
	4.2.2	Templates	☐		
	4.2.3	Macros	☐		
	4.2.4	Others	☐		
	Subcategory score				
4.3	**Configurable attributes**			**3.00**	
	4.3.1	Choice of plug-ins	☐		
	4.3.2	Browse options	☐		
	4.3.3	Indexes	☐		
	4.3.4	Sorting	☐		
	4.3.5	Preferences	☐		
	4.3.6	Metadata record display	☐		
	4.3.7	Image display	☐		
	Subcategory score				
4.4	**Display languages**			**2.00**	
	4.4.1	English	☐		

Categories		Weight	
4.4.2 Spanish	☐		
4.4.3 French	☐		
4.4.4 Other	☐		
Subcategory score			
Category: Flexibility total score			
5 Platform			**15%**
5.1 Client-server		4.00	
5.1.1 Client–server application	☐		
Subcategory score			
5.2 Client platform		2.00	
5.2.1 Windows XP	☐		
Subcategory score			
5.3 Server platform		4.00	
5.3.1 Unix and Unix-like OS	☐		
5.3.2 Apache web server	☐		
5.3.3 Perl API	☐		
5.3.4 Java API	☐		
5.3.5 Web service API	☐		
Subcategory score			
Category: Platform total score			
Technology total score			

Support

Categories		Weight	
1 Purchase/acquistion			**30%**
1.1 Trial and testing		4.00	
1.1.1 Download from website	☐		
1.1.2 Full-feature trial	☐		
Subcategory score			
1.2 Information		4.00	
1.2.1 Detailed information available online	☐		
1.2.2 Price listed	☐		
1.2.3 Detailed information available by phone	☐		
1.2.4 Contact information available online	☐		

Categories			Weight	
Subcategory score				
1.3	**Return/exchange**		**2.00**	
	1.3.1	Available	☐	
Subcategory score				
Category: Purchase/acquisition total score				
2	**Documentation**			**30%**
2.1	**User manual**		**4.00**	
	2.1.1	Online	☐	
	2.1.2	Include in the package	☐	
	2.1.3	Available for purchase	☐	
Subcategory score				
2.2	**Developer manual**		**3.00**	
	2.2.1	Online	☐	
	2.2.2	Include in the package	☐	
	2.2.3	Available for purchase	☐	
Subcategory score				
2.3	**Tutorials and examples**		**3.00**	
	2.3.1	Online	☐	
	2.3.2	Include in the package	☐	
Subcategory score				
Category: Documentation total score				
6	**Technical supports**			**20%**
3.1	**Online**		**4.00**	
	3.1.1	Online helpdesk	☐	
	3.1.2	User forum	☐	
	3.1.3	Discussion list	☐	
	3.1.4	Listserv	☐	
	3.1.5	E-mail contact	☐	
Subcategory score				
3.2	**By phone**		**3.00**	
	3.2.1	Dedicate technical support operator	☐	
	3.2.2	Available after hours	☐	
	3.2.3	Available on weekends	☐	
Subcategory score				

Categories		Weight	
3.3	**In person**	**1.00**	
	3.3.1 Available ☐		
	Subcategory score		
3.4	**Training**	**2.00**	
	3.4.1 Classes ☐		
	3.4.2 One by one ☐		
	Subcategory score		
	Category: Technical supports total score		
4	**Upgrading**		**20%**
	4.1 **Feature request system**	**4.00**	
	4.1.1 Request online ☐		
	4.1.2 Request by e-mail ☐		
	4.1.3 Request by formal writing ☐		
	Subcategory score		
	4.2 **Bug tracking**	**3.00**	
	4.2.1 With each release ☐		
	4.2.2 Available online ☐		
	Subcategory score		
	4.3 **Upgrading**	**3.00**	
	4.3.1 Easy to install ☐		
	Subcategory score		
	Category: Upgrading total score		
Support total score			

Organisational requirements and resources

1. Give a point between 1–5 (or 1–10) to a category in the 'O' table.

2. Assign a weight to each category (sample weights are assigned).

3. Multiply the point by the weight in each category to obtain the total score for each category.

4. Sum all total scores to obtain the final score for the 'O'.

5. Sum the 'FITS' score and the 'O' score to obtain the final score for each software package.

Categories	Point	Weight	Total score
Can handle most material types		20%	
Meet most user requirements		20%	
Within affordable budget		10%	
Compatible with current infrastructure		15%	
Has expertise to install and maintain		20%	
Can meet project schedule		5%	
Fit in strategic goals		10%	
Total		100%	

Appendix B:
Sample documentation from the WRLC Digital Collections Production Center

Sample 1: Digital collection project plan

June 4, 2003

Owner/repository:	American Catholic History Research Center and University Archives, Catholic University of America
Digital collection name:	The Brooks-Queen Family Collection
Collection description:	The Brooks-Queen Family Collection (1773–1979) consists of correspondence, holographic copies and extracts of correspondence, legal documents (many related to land transactions), treaty papers, essays, newspaper clippings, financial records, 'memorials' to Congress, notes, a Confederate government bond, and other papers spanning several generations. Some of the documents gathered here are present only as photocopies.
Collection scope:	Complete collection
Use restrictions:	None

Transfer of materials

	WRLC courier	Other
Delivery to WRLC:	_____	Deliver in person

Return to owning library: _____   Pick up in person

Project timeline (target dates)

Delivery of list of items and related information: Feb. 25, 2003

Delivery of finding aid in electronic form: Feb. 25, 2003 (Web)

Delivery of material to WRLC: May 5, 2003

Dublin Core template approval: June 13, 2003

Availability of DCPC preview site: Mid-July, 2003

Feedback for the preview site: End of July, 2003

Available to public: End of Sept. 2003

Contact person

Name: John Shepherd

        Phone: (202) 319 5065

        E-mail: *shepherw@cua.edu*

Sample 2: Copyright status document

June 2, 2003

Collection name: The Brooks-Queen Family Collection

Owner/repository: American Catholic History Research Center and University Archives, Catholic University of America

WRLC requires the owning library to affirm that it has the rights to digitise the material in this collection. In cases where works to be digitised are covered by copyright, the owning library is responsible for obtaining permission to digitise and disseminate the works from the copyright holder. A copy of the permissions document will be provided to WRLC along with the materials.

Please check the appropriate statement below.

___ To the best of our knowledge all the materials in this collection are in the public domain.

___ To the best of our knowledge all the materials in this collection are in the public domain with the exception of those on the attached list, for which copyright permission has been obtained (attached copy of permissions document(s)).

___ The materials in this collection are covered by copyright. Permission has been obtained from the copyright holder(s) (attach copy of permissions document(s)).

Signed: _____

Date: _____

Sample 3: Material characteristics and scanning specifications

The Brooks-Queen Family Collection

Source materials: About 1,500 pages of correspondence, holographic copies and extracts of correspondence, legal documents, treaty papers, essays, newspaper clippings, financial records, 'memorials' to Congress, notes, a Confederate government bond, and other papers spanning several generations. Some of the documents gathered here are present only as photocopies.

Scanning specifications

	Master	Display	Thumbnail
File format	TIFF	JPEG	JPEG
Scanning resolution	300 dpi		
Bit-depth	24-bit colour		
Compression	None	Medium	
Dimensions	Full size of the original	Various in size depending on the size of the original	150 pixels wide – landscape 150 pixels height – portrait

Sample 4: Dublin Core sample record

Photographic Material and Other Art Work of Herbert E. Striner

August 24, 2007

Dublin Core name	Example
DC.Title	Elderly man, Lafayette Park, Washington, DC (1966)
DC.Constributor	Striner, Herbert E., photographer
DC.Subject.persname	
DC.Subject	African American men – Washington (DC) – Photographs Urban elderly – Washington (DC) – Photographs Washington (DC) – Social life and customs – 1951- – Photographs
DC.Subject.corpname	Lafayette Park (Washington, DC) – Photographs
DC.Description	
DC.Description.notes	
DC.Date.created	1966
DC.Coverage.spatial	United States – District of Columbia – Washington
DC.Type	Images ‖ Photographs
DC.Source.extent	1 negative: b&w.; 35 mm.
DC.Language	en
Collection	Photographic Material and Other Art Work of Herbert E. Striner
DC.Rights	
DC.Source.repository	American University Library – University Archives
DC.Date.available	
Material Location	A001-23
WRLC.Capture.date	2007-08-27
WRLC.Capture.location	WRLC
WRLC.Capture.device	Epson Expression 1640XL
WRLC.Object.resolution	TIFF: 2,700 dpi
WRLC.Object.dimensions	JPEG: 600 pixels on long side
WRLC.Object.color	TIFF: 8-bit greyscale
WRLC.Object.compression	TIFF: none; JPEG: medium

Sample 5: Project summary and statistics

June 2005

American University History Photograph and Print Collection

Please use this URL for linking from your website or other places: *http://www.aladin.wrlc.org/dl/collection/hdr?auhist*

- *Date of completion*: May 2003. June 2005 (second batch)
- *Date of launch on the web*: May 19, 2003. June 29, 2005 (second batch)
- *Material returned*: March 14, 2003. June 30, 2005 (second batch).

Statistics

		Number
Images processed	TIFF	284 92 Total: 376
	JPEG	284 92 Total: 376
	Thumbnail	284 92 Total: 376
Text files produced	Text	
	HTML	
	PDF	
	Other	
DC records created		284 92 Total: 376
Webpages created		1
Master CD created		
Voyager record created (08/05/03)		1 (Bib ID: 6886500) (MFHD: audc)

Note

Two duplicate records were deleted in June 2005:

- Portrait of John Fletcher Hurst.
- Eleventh Commencement 1925.

Bibliography

Agnew, G. (2005) 'Developing a metadata strategy: a road map', *Journal of Digital Asset Management* 1(6): 372–85.

Albanese, A. R. (2007) 'Scan this book!', *Library Journal*, available at: *http://www.libraryjournal.com/article/CA6466634.html* (accessed 20 June 2008).

Arms, W. Y. (2000) *Digital Libraries*, Cambridge, MA: MIT Press.

Bauer, K. and Walls, D. (2005) 'DPIP priorities: needs, challenges, issues – workflow for digitization projects', available at: *http://www.library .yale.edu/iac/dpip/DPIPIssuesWorkflow.html* (accessed 23 March 2008).

Bekaert, J., Hochstenbach, P. and Van de Sompel, H. (2003) 'Using MPEG-21 DIDL to represent complex digital objects in the Los Alamos National Laboratory digital library', *D-Lib Magazine* 9(11), available at: *http://www.dlib.org/dlib/november03/bekaert/11bekaert.html* (accessed 23 March 2008).

Besser, H. (2003) *Introduction to Imaging* (revised edn), Los Angeles, CA: Getty Research Institute.

Caplan, P. (1995) 'You call it corn, we call it syntax-independent metadata for document-like objects', *The Public-Access Computer Systems Review* 6(4), available at: *http://epress.lib.uh.edu/pr/v6/n4/capl6n4 .html* (accessed 11 November 2007).

Chapman, S. (2000) 'Considerations for project management', in *Handbook for Digital Projects: A Management Tool for Preservation and Access*, available at: *http://nedcc.org/oldnedccsite/digital/dman2.pdf* (accessed 7 September 2007).

Choi, Y. and Rasmussen, E. (2006) 'What is needed to educate future digital librarians: a study of current practice and staffing patterns in academic and research libraries', *D-Lib Magazine* 12(9), available at: *http://www.dlib.org/dlib/september06/choi/09choi.html* (accessed 22 March 2008).

Clareson, T. (2006) 'NEDCC survey and colloquium explore digitization and digital preservation policies and practices', *RLG DigiNews* 10(1), available at: *http://digitalarchive.oclc.org/da/ViewObjectMain.jsp? objid=0000068991&reqid=302&frame=true* (accessed 20 June 2008).

Connecticut History Online (CHO) (2000) 'Picturing the past for students of the future: Connecticut History Online', available at: *http://www.cthistoryonline.org/cdm-cho/cho/project/press-release.htm* (accessed 18 July 2008).

Connecticut History Online (CHO) (2001) 'Project description', available at: *http://www.cthistoryonline.org/cdm-cho/cho/project/ Abstract.htm* (accessed 18 July 2008).

Cornell University Library (2005) 'Selecting traditional library materials for digitization: report of the CUL Task Force on Digitization', available at: *http://www.library.cornell.edu/colldev/digitalselection.html* (accessed 27 November 2007).

Coyle, K. and Hillmann, D. (2007) 'Resource description and access (RDA): cataloging rules for the 20th century', *D-Lib Magazine* 13(1/2), available at: *http://www.dlib.org/dlib/january07/coyle/01coyle.html* (accessed 1 December 2007).

Dahl, M., Banerjee, K. and Spalti, M. (2006) *Digital Libraries: Integrating Content and Systems*, Oxford: Chandos Publishing.

Dilauro, T. (2004) 'Choosing the components of a digital infrastructure', *First Monday* 9(5), available at: *http://firstmonday.org/issues/issue9_5/ dilauro/index.html* (accessed 14 September 2007).

Dublin Core Metadata Initiative (DCMI) (2006) 'DCMI metadata terms', available at: *http://dublincore.org/documents/dcmi-terms/#H2* (accessed 30 November 2007).

El-Sherbini, M. and Klim, G. (2004) 'Metadata and cataloging practices', *The Electronic Library* 22(3): 238–48.

Erway, R. and Schaffner, J. (2007) 'Shifting gears: gearing up to get into the flow. Report produced by OCLC Programs and Research', available at: *www.oclc.org/programs/publications/reports/2007-02.pdf* (accessed 20 June 2008).

Fulton, W. (1997) 'A few scanning tips', available at: *http://www.scantips .com/* (accessed 27 March 2008).

Goh, D. H., Chua, A., Khoo, D. A., Khoo, E. B., Mak, E. B. and Ng, M. W. (2006) 'A checklist for evaluating open source digital library software', *Online Information Review* 30(4): 360–79.

Gourley, D. (2007) 'DSpace as a platform: creating custom interfaces with content packaging plugins', paper presented at the DSpace User Group, Open Repositories 2007, San Antonio, TX, 23–26 January, available at: *http://dspace.wrlc.org/doc/wrlc/DSpaceAsAPlatform.pdf* (accessed 10 March 2008).

Gradmann, S. (1998) 'Cataloguing vs. metadata: old wine in new bottles?', available at: *http://www.ifla.org/IV/ifla64/007-126e.htm* (accessed 9 February 2008).

Han, Y. (2004) 'Digital content management: the search for a content management system', *Library Hi Tech* 22(4): 355–65.

Hartman, C., Belden, D., Reis, N., Alemneh, D., Phillips, M. and Dunlop, D. (2005) 'Development of a portal to Texas history', *Library Hi Tech* 23(2): 151–63.

Hazen, D., Horrell, J. and Merrill-Oldham, J. (1998) 'Selecting research collections for digitization', available at: *http://www.clir.org/pubs/reports/hazen/pub74.html* (accessed 29 September 2007).

Hedstrom, M. (2001) 'Digital preservation: problems and prospects', *Digital Libraries* 20, available at: *http://www.dl.slis.tsukuba.ac.jp/DLjournal/No_20/1-hedstrom/1-hedstrom.html* (accessed 29 September 2007).

Hillmann, D. (2005) 'Using Dublin Core', available at: *http://dublincore.org/documents/usageguide/* (accessed 30 November 2007).

Hinderliter, H. (2003) 'The basics of a scanned image', *SilverFast: The Official Guide*, Alameda, CA: Sybex, Inc.

Hughes, L. M. (2004) *Digitizing Collections: Strategic Issues for the Information Manager*, London: Facet Publishing.

International Children's Digital Library (2005) 'Collection development policy', available at: *http://www.icdlbooks.org/about/collection.shtml* (accessed 15 February 2008).

International Organization for Standardization (ISO) (2003) *Space data and information transfer systems – Open archival information system – Reference model*, Geneva: ISO.

Jayakanth, F. (2007) 'Institutional repository software: features and functionalities', available at: *http://casin.ncsi.iisc.ernet.in/workshop/jul252707/presentations/IR_Software.pdf* (accessed 23 March 2008).

Jerrido, M., Cotilla, L. and Whitehead, T. (2001) 'Digitizing collections: a meshing of minds, methods, and materials', *Collection Management* 26(3): 3–13.

Joint Steering Committee for Development of RDA (2007) 'RDA: Resource Description and Access', available at: *http://www.collectionscanada.ca/jsc/rda.html* (accessed 20 July 2008).

Kahn, R. and Wilensky, R. (1995) 'A framework for distributed digital object services', available at: *http://www.cnri.reston.va.us/k-w.html* (accessed 4 November 2007).

Kenney, A. R. and Rieger, O. Y. (2000) *Moving Theory into Practice: Digital Imaging for Libraries and Archives*, Mountain View, CA: Research Libraries Group.

Kenney, A. R., Rieger, O. Y. and Entlich, R. (2002) 'Moving theory into practice: digital imaging tutorial', available at: *http://www.library .cornell.edu/preservation/tutorial/* (accessed 29 September 2007).

Lane, T. (1995) 'JPEG image compression FAQ', available at: *http:// www.faqs.org/faqs/jpeg-faq/part1/* (accessed 30 December 2007).

Library of Congress (1999) 'Ameritech National Digital Library Competition (1996–1999): Lessons learned: workflow and project management', available at: *http://memory.loc.gov/ammem/award/ lessons/workflow.html* (accessed 20 July 2008).

Library of Congress Authorities (2008) 'Frequently asked questions', available at: *http://authorities.loc.gov/help/auth-faq.htm#1* (accessed 18 July 2008).

Lopatin, L. (2006) 'Library digitization projects, issues and guidelines: a survey of the literature', *Library Hi Tech* 24(2): 273–89.

Lynch, C. (2002) 'Digital collections, digital libraries and the digitization of cultural heritage information', *First Monday* 7(5), available at: *http://firstmonday.org/issues/issue7_5/lynch/index.html* (accessed 25 August 2007).

McDonald, J. (2003) 'A recipe for a successful digital archive: collection development for digital archives', *Against the Grain* 15(1): 22–4.

Miller, A. P. (1996) 'Metadata for the masses', available at: *http://www .ariadne.ac.uk/issue5/metadata-masses/* (accessed 26 March 2008).

Moving Image Collections (2007) 'Glossary of cataloging & general terms', available at: *http://gondolin.rutgers.edu/MIC/text/how/catalog_ glossary.htm* (accessed 30 November 2007).

National Archives and Records Administration (NARA) (2004) 'Technical guidelines for digitizing archival materials for electronic access: creation of production master files – raster images', available at: *http://www.archives.gov/preservation/technical/guidelines.html* (accessed 18 July 2008).

National Initiative for a Networked Cultural Heritage (2002) 'The NINCH guide to good practice in the digital representation and management of cultural heritage materials', available at: *http://www.nyu.edu/its/ humanities/ninchguide/* (accessed 29 September 2007).

National Library of Australia (year unknown) 'Digitisation', available at: *http://www.nla.gov.au/padi/topics/69.html* (accessed 7 September 2007).

Nielsen, J. (2005) 'Ten usability heuristics', available at: *http://www .useit.com/papers/heuristic/heuristic_list.html* (accessed 1 March 2008).

Nielsen, J. (2008) 'User skills improving, but only slightly', available at: *http://www.useit.com/alertbox/user-skills.html* (accessed 8 March 2008).

Nielsen, J. and Loranger, H. (2006) *Prioritizing Web Usability*, Berkeley, CA: New Riders.

Nielsen, J. and Tahir, M. (2002) *Homepage Usability: 50 Websites Deconstructed*, Indianapolis, IN: New Riders.

NISO Framework Advisory Group (2004) *A Framework of Guidance for Building Good Digital Collections* (2nd edn), Bethesda, MD: National Information Standards Organization.

Open Source Initiative (2007) 'Home', available at: *http://www.opensource.org/* (accessed 20 July 2008).

Open Society Institute (2004) *A Guide to Institutional Repository Software* (3rd edn), available at: *http://www.soros.org/openaccess/software/OSI_Guide_to_Institutional_Repository_Software_v3.htm* (accessed 20 July 2008).

Payne, E. A. (2001) 'Proposal to Institute of Museum and Library Services: 2001 National Leadership Grants for Libraries', available at: *http://www.wrlc.org/diglib/dcpc/imlsproposal.pdf* (accessed 8 March 2008).

Payne, E. A. (2004) 'WRLC Digital Collections Production Center (DCPC) Guidebook', available at: *http://www.wrlc.org/diglib/dcpc/Services/documents/dcpcguidebook.pdf* (accessed 18 July 2008).

Porter, M. E. (1985) *Competitive Advantage*. New York, NY: The Free Press.

Raymond, E. S. (1999) *The Cathedral and the Bazaar*, Cambridge, MA: O'Reilly Media.

Robertson, J. (2002) 'How to evaluate a content management system', available at: *http://www.steptwo.com.au/papers/kmc_evaluate/* (accessed 20 September 2007).

Rosenthal, D. S. H., Robertson, T., Lipkis, T., Reich, V. and Morabito, S. (2005) 'Requirements for digital preservation systems', *D-Lib Magazine* 11(11), available at: *http://www.dlib.org/dlib/november05/rosenthal/11rosenthal.html* (accessed 10 March 2008).

Rossmann, B. and Rossmann, D. (2005) 'Communication with library systems support personnel: models for success', *Library Philosophy and Practice* 7(2), available at: *http://www.webpages.uidaho.edu/~mbolin/rossmann.htm* (accessed 18 July 2008).

Rusbridge, C. (2006) 'Excuse me... some digital preservation fallacies?', *Ariadne* 45, available at: *http://www.ariadne.ac.uk/issue46/rusbridge/* (accessed 10 March 2008).

Savyak, V. (2002) 'iSCSI Review', available at: *http://www.digit-life.com/articles2/iscsi/* (accessed 20 July 2008).

Shatford, S. (1986) 'Analyzing the subject of picture: a theoretical approach', *Cataloging & Classification Quarterly* 6(3): 39–62.

Singh, S. (2005) 'Gathering the stories behind our statistics', *American Libraries* 36(10): 46–8.

Smith, A. (2001) *Strategies for Building Digitized Collection*, Washington, DC: Digital Library Federation, Council on Library and Information Resources.

Smith, A. (2003) 'Issues in sustainability: creating value for online users', *First Monday* 8(5), available at: *http://firstmonday.org/issues/issue8_5/smith/index.html* (accessed 20 June 2008).

Smith-Yoshimura, K. (2007) 'RLG programs descriptive metadata practices survey results', available at: *www.oclc.org/programs/publications/reports/2007-03.pdf* (accessed 1 March 2008).

SMETE Digital Library (1999) 'Vision statement', available at: *http://www.smete.org/smete/?path=/public/about_smete/vision_statement/index.jhtml&* (accessed 1 March 2008).

Society of American Archivists (2004) 'Describing Archives: A Content Standard (DACS)', available at: *http://www.archivists.org/governance/standards/dacs.asp;* (accessed 7 December 2007).

Surman, M. and Diceman, J. (2004), 'Choosing open source: a guide for civil society organizations', available at: *http://www.commons.ca/articles/fulltext.shtml?x=335* (accessed 20 July 2008).

Tally, T. (2003) *SilverFast: The Official Guide*, Alameda, CA: Sybex.

Tanner, S. (2001) 'Librarians in the digital age: planning digitisation projects', *Program* 35(4), available at: *http://www.aslib.co.uk/program/protected/2001/oct/01.pdf* (accessed 28 October 2007).

Tansley, R., Bass, M., Stuve, D., Branschofsky, M., Chudnov, D., McClellan, G. and Smith, M. (2003) 'The DSpace institutional digital repository system: current functionality', in *ACM/IEEE 2003 Joint Conference on Digital Libraries: Proceedings*, Los Alamitos, CA: IEEE Computer Society.

Tognazzini, B. (2007) 'First principles of interaction design', available at: *http://www.asktog.com/basics/firstPrinciples.html* (accessed 12 December 2007).

Umbach, J. M. (2001) 'Talking to techies', *Feliciter* 47(5): 234–5.

Vogt-O'Connor, D. (2005) 'Selection of materials for scanning', in *Conservation Center's Handbook for Digital Project*, available at: *http://www.nedcc.org/oldnedccsite/digital/iv.htm#intro* (accessed 20 September 2007).

Von Hippel, E. and von Krogh, G. (2003) 'Open source software and the 'private-collective' innovation model: issues for organization science', *Organization Science*, 14(2): 209–23.

Wendler, R. (1999) 'LDI update: metadata in the library', *Library Note*, Boston, MA: Harvard University.

Western States Digital Standards Group (2003) 'Western States digital imaging best practices', available at: *http://www.bcr.org/cdp/best/digital-imaging-bp.pdf* (accessed 29 March 2008).

Wisser, K. M. (ed.) (2005) 'Guidelines for digitization', available at: *http://www.ncecho.org/Guide/toc.htm* (accessed 4 November 2007).

Witten, I. H., Bainbridge, D., Tansley, R., Huang, C. and Don, K. J. (2005) 'StoneD: A bridge between Greenstone and DSpace', *D-Lib Magazine*, 11(9), available at: *http://www.dlib.org/dlib/september05/witten/09witten.html* (accessed 22 March 2008).

Zhang, B. A. (1996) *File Formats on the Internet: A Guide for PC Users*, Washington DC: Special Libraries Association.

Zhang, B. A. (2007) 'Creating online historical scrapbooks with a user-friendly interface: a case study', *D-Lib Magazine* 13(11/12), available at: *http://www.dlib.org/dlib/november07/zhang/11zhang.html* (accessed 22 March 2008).

Zhang, B. A. and Gourley, D. (2003) 'A digital collections management system based on open source software', in *ACM/IEEE 2003 Joint Conference on Digital Libraries: Proceedings*, Los Alamitos, CA: IEEE Computer Society.

Index

Printed in the United States
145576LV00002B/1/P

9 781843 343967